HELLO MOONCHILD!

How wonderful that you are here and that you exist in this universe.
I see you, I feel you, and I'm so delighted to accompany you on your journey this year.
Within you burns a unique spark, a magic that only you can share with the world. Let it shine brightly!
Discover the boundless strength within you and the infinite love that lies at the core of your being.
From the bottom of my heart, I wish for all your dreams to come true and for you to embrace the full depth of your unique path in life.
I'm already looking forward to creating magical moments with you, igniting your inner spark, and spreading enchantment together!
Let's make the world a little brighter, more fulfilling, and more beautiful.
You are part of something grand, yet unmistakably one of a kind.
Never forget how much light you carry within you and how deeply you enrich the world with it.

NO MATTER WHERE YOU ARE RIGHT NOW, YOU ARE EXACTLY
WHERE YOU'RE MEANT TO BE.
NO MATTER HOW YOU FEEL, YOU ARE WHOLE AND
COMPLETE.
NO MATTER WHAT YOU THINK, IT'S VALID, BUT NOT ALWAYS
THE TRUTH.
EVEN WHEN EVERYTHING FEELS OVERPOWERING, BELIEVE IN
YOURSELF.

THIS BOOK
BELONGS TO

_____

_____

_____

Table of Contents

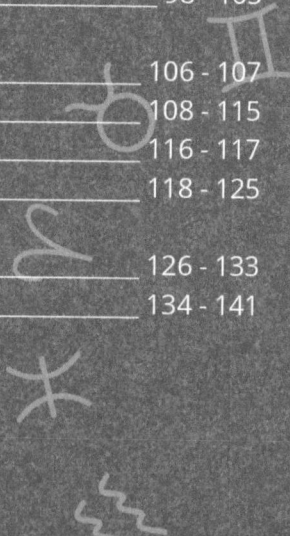

Table of Contents

LET'S MAKE THIS YEAR TRULY SPECIAL!

—————›››‹ o·· ◇ o··— -THE UNIVERSE

2025

● Full Moon ✪ Luna Eclipse
○ New Moon ✦ Solar Eclipse

January

M	T	W	T	F	S	S
		1	2	3	4	5
6	7	8	11	12	●	14
15	16	17	18	19	20	21
22	23	24	25	26	27	28
㉙	30	31				

February

M	T	W	T	F	S	S
				1	2	3	4
5	6	7	8	9	10	11
●	13	14	15	16	17	18
19	20	21	22	23	24	25
26	27	㉘	29			

March

M	T	W	T	F	S	S
					1	2	3
4	5	6	7	8	9	10
11	12	13	✪	15	16	17
18	19	20	21	22	23	24
25	26	27	28	✦	30	31

April

M	T	W	T	F	S	S
1	2	3	4	5	6	7
8	9	10	11	12	●	14
15	16	17	18	19	20	21
22	23	24	25	26	㉗	28
29	30					

May

M	T	W	T	F	S	S
			1	2	3	4	5
6	7	8	9	10	11	●
13	14	15	16	17	18	19
20	21	22	23	24	25	26
㉗	28	29	30	31		

June

M	T	W	T	F	S	S
					1	2
3	4	5	6	7	8	9
10	●	12	13	14	15	16
17	18	19	20	21	22	23
24	㉕	26	27	28	29	30

July

M	T	W	T	F	S	S
1	2	3	4	5	6	7
8	9	10	●	12	13	14
15	16	17	18	19	20	21
22	23	㉔	25	26	27	28
29	30	31				

August

M	T	W	T	F	S	S
				1	2	3	4
5	6	7	8	●	10	11
12	13	14	15	16	17	18
19	20	21	22	㉓	24	25
26	27	28	29	30	31	

September

M	T	W	T	F	S	S
						1
2	3	4	5	6	✪	8
9	10	11	12	13	14	15
16	17	18	19	20	✦	22
23/30	24	25	26	27	28	29

October

M	T	W	T	F	S	S
	1	2	3	4	5	6
●	8	9	10	11	12	13
14	15	16	17	18	19	20
㉑	22	23	24	25	26	27
28	29	30	31			

November

M	T	W	T	F	S	S
					1	2	3
4	●	6	7	8	9	10
11	12	13	14	15	16	17
18	19	⑳	21	22	23	24
25	26	27	28	29	30	

December

M	T	W	T	F	S	S
						1
2	3	4	●	6	7	8
9	10	11	12	13	14	15
16	17	18	19	⑳	21	22
23/30	24/31	25	26	27	28	29

THE FASCINATING AND CAPTIVATING MOON
OUR SPIRITUAL GUIDE

While the moon is masculine in my native German language, it is feminine in many others. This is because the moon symbolically represents the feminine, intuition, emotions, and the subconscious. Whether viewed as a mystical symbol, a cause of restless nights, or a natural phenomenon, the moon holds a magical fascination for us.

It moves the seas, so it's no wonder it moves us too. The rhythm of the moon reminds us of the natural ebb and flow of life, and its energy is deeply connected to our inner selves. **Living in harmony with the moon's phases can help us navigate life's waves more consciously and with greater purpose.** The moon's various phases throughout the month bring unique energies and serve as a guide, aligning us with cycles of growth, release, and renewal. It can help us act at the right moments, let go, or start afresh.

THE MOON PHASES AND CHARACTERISTICS

1. New Moon – The New Beginning

The New Moon marks the start of a new lunar cycle. It represents fresh starts, renewed energy, and the chance to set new intentions. This is a time to tune into your inner desires and reflect on what you wish to manifest in your life. New Moon energy is calm and supportive—the perfect moment to initiate something new.

- *Energy*: Calmness, clarity, anticipation, fresh beginnings
- *Focus:* Manifestation, setting intentions
- *Spiritual Impulse*: Connect with your core, visualise your dreams, and take the first steps towards your future

2. Waxing Moon – Growth and Building

As the moon grows fuller, not only do our emotions intensify, but we are also encouraged to transform our energy into motivation. This is the phase for action and implementation. Focus on pursuing your dreams and desires, and work on bringing your plans to reality. This phase symbolises growth, progress, and determination.

- *Energy*: Building, movement, progress, purpose
- *Focus*: Implementing plans, advancing projects
- *Spiritual Impulse*: Stay focused and connected to your highest self

3. Full Moon – Climax and Letting Go

The Full Moon is the powerful and magical highlight of the lunar cycle. Emotions run high, and everything hidden in the shadows is brought to light. This is the phase of letting go, clarity, and fulfilment. If you manifest your desires during the New Moon, you see the results or recognise what's holding you back from achieving them. It's a time to release what no longer serves you and celebrate what you've accomplished.

- *Energy*: Intensity, fulfilment, letting go
- *Focus*: Completion, reflection, clarity
- *Spiritual Impulse*: Release old patterns, fears, and blockages, and celebrate your successes

4. Waning Moon – Retreat and Reflection

After the intensity of the full moon, the phase of retreat begins. As the moon wanes, our emotions start to settle. This is a time for reflection, pausing, and preparing for the next cycle. It's also a chance to complete tasks you've already started. The waning moon phase is ideal for healing, introspection, and processing the past few weeks.

- *Energy*: Calmness, retreat, reflection, endings
- *Focus:* Healing, tidying up, completion, letting go
- *Spiritual Impulse*: Allow yourself to rest and prepare to start the cycle anew

The moon's cycle reminds us that life comprises of phases – times for growth and action and times for retreat and healing.
By living in harmony with your energy levels and the moons phases, you use your energy more effectively and align with the natural rhythms of your life, not feeling you have to give 100% at all times. Each phase of the moon offers a unique opportunity to connect with yourself and consciously embrace your spiritual journey.

New Moon: Start something new.
Waxing Moon: Build upon it.
Full Moon: Let go of what no longer serves you.
Waning Moon: Turn inward and heal.

THE MOON IN THE ZODIAC SIGNS

The Moon moves through the different zodiac signs every 2–3 days, adopting the qualities of each sign as it passes. **This means that the energy we feel is heavily influenced by the zodiac sign the Moon is currently in.** These shifts affect our emotions, motivation, and interactions with the world around us.

Each zodiac sign carries its unique energy and focus:

Fire Signs
(Aries, Leo, Sagittarius)
bring bold, energetic, and determined vibes.

Earth Signs
(Taurus, Virgo, Capricorn)
are grounded, practical, and focused on stability.

Air Signs
(Gemini, Libra, Aquarius)
promote communication, intellect, and social interactions.

Water Signs
(Cancer, Scorpio, Pisces)
emphasise emotions, intuition, and deep inner processes.

Depending on the phase of the Moon (New Moon or Full Moon), these zodiac signs have varying influences on us.

When the **New Moon** is in a particular sign, that sign's energy shapes new beginnings. For example, a New Moon in Aries brings powerful energy for taking bold steps and starting new projects, while a New Moon in Virgo inspires you to organise your life and create structure.

A **Full Moon** amplifies the energy of the sign it's in. A Full Moon in Scorpio can be intense, emotional, and transformative, perfect for releasing deeply rooted feelings. A Full Moon in Libra, on the other hand, focuses on relationships and harmony, inviting you to find balance in your life.

The zodiac sign the Moon occupies provides an energetic framework for the themes we can focus on during that Moon cycle—whether it's releasing during the Full Moon or manifesting during the New Moon.

Think of the Moon as your guide and companion, reminding you that change, growth and healing are always possible. Use the energy to check in with yourself every two weeks through a meaningful ritual, create your dream life, and bring magic into your world.

YOUR FULL MOON RITUAL

Everyone knows it – emotions run high, we feel more intensely, sleep worsens, and everything suddenly seems so much more extreme. Yes, it's the Full Moon! The **energy of the Full Moon** marks the peak of the lunar cycle and urges us to clean up – both internally and externally. The Full Moon brings our deepest feelings and thoughts to the surface, some of which we may not have been aware of. It's the perfect time to shed baggage and release everything that holds us back.

This is precisely why a Full Moon ritual should be a magical opportunity to **eliminate all that no longer serves us**. Negative vibes, bad habits, old emotions – everything can be appropriately burned (safely, of course!) and released under the Full Moon. But that's not all: you can also take a moment to be genuinely proud of yourself and pat yourself on the back for what you've accomplished. Acknowledge everything you've already achieved and celebrate gratitude.

Under the light of the Full Moon, we free ourselves, creating a void and, thus, space for new things. That's why it's important to fill this space with emotions that serve us and keep our vibrations high. Love, gratitude, and joy are part of this. See the Full Moon as the halftime of your manifestations and as a reset button for your attraction power!

The intensity of the Full Moon makes us feel more deeply, so use it! The Full Moon celebrates you, so celebrate yourself too!

The Full Moon Energy :
- *Overdose of Emotion*: Yes, it can get emotional. Tears, laughter, everything is in there. The Full Moon amplifies everything!
- *Detox*: Think of it as a spiritual decluttering. Clear your mind and heart to make space for new, better things. Whether you want to eliminate an old habit or stop overthinking everything – now is the time for it.
- *Gratitude*: Take a moment to look at everything you've achieved! It's time to see the glass half full and throw a big gratitude party. Celebrate your successes, even if it's "I wore two matching socks today."

THE ROADMAP
OF YOUR FULL MOON RITUAL

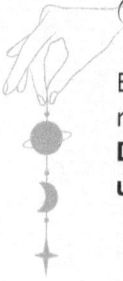

Every full moon ritual has a similar flow – that's what makes it a ritual, right?! Below, you'll find the general structure and critical points. **Depending on which zodiac sign the full moon is in, it will have a unique energy and focus on specific themes.**

- **Make yourself comfortable**: Light a few candles or incense, and ensure you won't be disturbed. Play some soothing background music, snuggle up with your favourite blanket, and gather your supplies (pen, paper, crystals, essential oils, etc.).

- **Arrive in the present moment**: Close your eyes, take a deep breath, and feel the gentle energy of the full moon surrounding you. Let go of any stress – it might take a moment, but you've got this! Take your time with the reflection and journalling questions, and notice how your energy begins to align with the moon's.

- **Let go with intention**: Write down what you'd like to release, letting it all flow onto the paper. Then, in a safe space, perform your burning ritual. Watch your worries transform into smoke and feel the freedom as they fade away.

- **Express gratitude**: You've created emotional space. After releasing what no longer serves you, take a moment to write down all the things you're grateful for. Every little thing matters. Fill the space you've created with gratitude and warmth.

- **Make room for special touches**: Each full moon offers small rituals and practices that can complement your ritual. There are no rules – enjoy the time for yourself and do what feels right in your heart.

- **Chakra meditation**: Close the ritual by spending a few minutes focusing on your breathing and inviting positive energy. You can incorporate the affirmation of the current moon and gently repeat it in your mind. Visualise yourself feeling light, free, and renewed.

HIDDEN GEM: CHAKRA MEDITATION

Chakra meditation is a practice that focuses on the seven energy centers in the body. These chakras are meditation points along the spine, from the base to the crown of the head, and represent different aspects of our lives and consciousness. Each chakra is associated with a colour, an element, specific affirmations, and a mantra.

By directing focus and energy to the meditation points, you can help harmonise the energy centres in your body, release any blockages, and encourage the natural flow of energy. Through mindful meditation on each chakra, using soothing visualisations (like the corresponding colour), affirmations, and breathing exercises, you can support the balance of your chakras. This practice can guide you towards spiritual growth, emotional healing, and a deeper connection with yourself.

WHAT THE CHAKRA?

1. Root Chakra

Colour: Red
Element: Earth
Affirmations: "I am..."
Main Themes: Vitality, Stability, Trust
Activities: Walking barefoot, movement
Mantra: Lam

2. Sacral Chakra

Colour: Orange
Element: Water
Affirmations: "I feel..."
Main Themes: Surrender, Sexuality, Intuition, Creativity
Activities: Swimming, painting, creative activities
Mantra: Vam

HIDDEN GEM: CHAKRA MEDITATION
WHAT THE CHAKRA?

3. Solar Plexus Chakra

Colour: Yellow
Element: Fire
Affirmations: "I can..."
Main Themes: Clarity, Wisdom, Self-confidence
Activities: Sunbathing, fireplace, candlelight dinner
Mantra: Ram

4. Heart Chakra

Colour: Green
Element: Air
Affirmations: "I love..."
Main Themes: Compassion, Love, Freedom, Connection
Activities: Pampering yourself, caring for pets
Mantra: Yam

5. Throat Chakra

Colour: Light Blue
Element: Ether (Space)
Affirmations: "I speak..."
Main Themes: Authenticity, Communication, Inner Growth
Activities: Singing, Writing, Music
Mantra: Ham

6. Third Eye Chakra

Colour: Indigo Blue
Element: Light
Affirmations: "I see..."
Main Themes: Emotional Intelligence, Spirituality
Activities: Journalling dreams, Meditating
Mantra: Sham

7. Crown Chakra

Colour: Violet
Element: Cosmic Energy
Affirmations: "I understand..."
Main Themes: Self-awareness, Spirituality, Higher Knowledge
Activities: Hiking, Scenery and Broader Perspective
Mantra: Om

HIDDEN GEM: CHAKRA MEDITATION
ROADMAP FOR THE MEDITATION

1. **Preparation:** Find a quiet and peaceful spot, close your eyes, and bring your attention to your breath. Take a deep, calming inhale and exhale, allowing yourself to *relax* and *become still*.

2. **Visualisation**: Gently focus on the area of your body where your chakra is located. Picture a *soft, glowing ball* of energy and light in the colour of the *chakra* resting there.

3. **Breathing and Energy Flow**: Take a slow, deep breath, guiding the energy to the chakra area. With each *inhale*, imagine the light and energy *growing stronger* in this space. As you *exhale*, allow any tension or *blockages to melt away gently*. Feel the light expanding with each breath, filling your body until a warm, *glowing sphere surrounds you*.

4. **Closing and Integration:** When you're ready to finish, imagine the *energy from the chakra flowing smoothly through your entire body*, gently surrounding and nourishing you. Take a deep breath in and out, rest your hands over the chakra area, and repeat calming *affirmations* that resonate with that chakra. When you're ready, slowly open your eyes and notice how the energy feels within you. You can also gently bring the energy back to the chakra by softly repeating or singing the corresponding mantra.

YOUR NEW MOON RITUAL

The New Moon and the dark night sky are like a blank canvas. **It's the perfect time to set your inner desires and visions into motion**. While the Full Moon urges you to let go of the old, the New Moon offers the chance to **bring fresh energy into your life**. The New Moon is your personal launchpad – filled with fresh energy, inspiration, and endless possibilities. So, if you want to manifest something, now is the right moment! A New Moon ritual helps you sort your thoughts, set your intentions, and direct your energy towards the path you want to take. Whether it's about your career, relationships, or personal journey – the New Moon is the starting signal. **Manifest, dream big, and get ready for miracles!**

The New Moon Energy:
- *"Anything-is-possible" vibe*: The universe is hitting the reset button – use this opportunity to start fresh.
- *Manifestation*: Now is the moment to send your goals and wishes out into the universe—no limitations, no old patterns, just a blank canvas where you can create your new masterpiece. Set clear intentions: What do you truly want to attract into your life? Now is the perfect time to begin.
- *Vision*: The future lies before you – so what do you want to make of it? See it, feel it, believe in it – and let it happen.

THE ROADMAP
FOR YOUR NEW MOON RITUAL

Each New Moon ritual follows a gentle flow, with the main focus being manifestation. Here's a simple outline to guide you.

The energy of the New Moon changes depending on the zodiac sign it's in, offering unique support for manifesting your desires in different ways.

1. Create a Calm Atmosphere: Light some candles, make yourself comfortable, and play soft, inspiring music in the background. Ensure you have everything you need – a journal, your favourite crystals, or a cosy blanket.

2. Centre Yourself: Take a few deep breaths and feel the calm energy of the New Moon. Imagine the dark sky gently surrounding you, filling you with a sense of peace and limitless possibilities. Reflect on your intentions through the journal prompts.

3. Gratitude Ritual: Take a moment to write down things you are grateful for in your life. As you focus on the things that bring you joy, you naturally raise your vibration, making it easier to attract more positive things into your life.

4. Manifestation Ritual: This is where the magic happens – grab a pen and write down your deepest dreams and desires. No wish is too big or small if you believe in it. Visualise yourself already living the life you dream of. Feel the happiness, the freedom, the joy – let your manifestations unfold in your mind.

5. Creative Manifestation and Visualisation: Engage in a few light, creative tasks (everything is optional, nothing is required) to deepen your visualisation and help you connect with your desires. Trust your intuition and let the New Moon guide you with gentle energy.

6. Meditation and Letting Go: Sit quietly for a few moments and meditate. A simple chakra meditation can help you centre your energy and connect with your higher self. Let go of any attachments to your vision, knowing that the universe is already working to bring your desires to life. When you're ready, return to the present moment, feeling at peace with the process.

HIDDEN GEM: MANIFESTING
WHAT TO DO

Manifesting means consciously bringing what you desire into your life. It's about aligning your thoughts, emotions, and actions with a specific goal. Here's a simple step-by-step guide to manifesting successfully:

1. Create Clarity: What do you really want?
The first step is to clarify your desires. Ask yourself questions like: What do I want to have or achieve in my life? How do I want to feel? *Be specific!* The universe can only deliver what you truly ask for, so pay attention to the important *details*.
Example: Instead of saying, "I want pasta," try: "I eat ravioli stuffed with mushrooms and spinach in a tomato-basil sauce, topped with a sprinkle of Parmesan."

2. Set Your Intention: Frame your wish positively
Now that you know what you want focus on what you truly desire rather than what you want to avoid. Your focus should be positive. Formulate your wish in *clear, positive statements*, using the *present tense* as if your desire has already come true. This sends the signal to your subconscious that it's already part of your life.
Example: Instead of saying, "I don't want a boring 9-5 job," say: "I am a happy and successful author, working on my regular projects remotely and on my own schedule."

Important: Clear, positive statements are more powerful. Vague wishes or doubts make manifestation harder.

3. Visualise: Imagine your wish is already a reality
The most powerful part of manifestation is visualisation. Close your eyes and vividly imagine what it would be like if your wish had already come true. Mentally put yourself in that situation—how do you feel? What do you see, hear, smell, and, most importantly, feel? *The stronger you can feel it, the more energy you're giving to your manifestation.*

4. Faith and Trust: Be convinced that it will work

Manifesting requires *trust*. You must firmly believe that your desire can and will come true. Doubts and negative thoughts block the process. Trust that the universe or your inner power will support you and make your wishes come true. Avoid thoughts like "What if it doesn't work?" or "I wish, but.." – instead, *stay positive and confident.*

5. Gratitude: Be grateful as if your wish has already come true

Gratitude is a powerful tool in manifestation. Gratitude puts you in a *high frequency* and signals to the universe that you are ready to receive more. Every day, give thanks for what you already have and what is coming to you – as if it is already here.

Important: Feelings are the key – manifesting is the feeling you experience when your wish comes true. Positive emotions like joy, gratitude, and love amplify the power of manifestation. Keep your vibration high and bring those feelings into your daily life.

6. Letting Go: Give the universe room to work

After setting your intention, visualising and feeling it, comes the most challenging part: *letting go.* Release the urge to control things and trust that the right time and opportunities will come. *Too much pressure creates resistance.* Letting go doesn't mean giving up on your desire but *trusting* the universe and being open to unexpected paths and opportunities.

Important: You don't need to know how your desire will be fulfilled – just trust that it will. Some wishes take time to unfold. Keep your focus, and don't lose faith. Everything happens at the right time.

13.01.2025
CANCER
FULL MOON

FULL MOON
IN CANCER

Drumroll, please! It's time: The very first Full Moon of 2025 is here, ready to gift us the perfect fresh start to the year! Forget about New Year's resolutions and your "New Year, New Me" mantra, which might have wobbled a bit or been completely abandoned in the first few days. This Full Moon offers you a chance to start over - and this time, differently.

In the **emotional** and **cosy** sign of Cancer, this Full Moon delivers a clear message: **don't stress yourself out**. Put on your favourite cuddly socks and tend to your **inner sanctuary** and **well-being**. After likely spending Christmas and New Year surrounded by family and friends (and perhaps navigating some awkward dinner conversations), it's time to hit the **emotional reset button**. Are you feeling like you're on an emotional rollercoaster? Let it happen! It's okay if the feelings overflow. Grab the tissues, watch a cheesy rom-com, and let it all out. Sometimes, a good cry is just what's needed!

What does this Full Moon bring?

This Full Moon invites you to confront your deepest **emotions**. What do you truly need to feel **safe** and **secure**? It's okay to take a break from the world - and maybe even Aunty Gladys' constant questions about your love life. Remember, she probably didn't mean any harm, so let it go.

Focus:

Have you been giving yourself enough **self-love** lately? This is your moment to focus on what truly nourishes you emotionally. Family, friends, your **inner balance** - anything that makes you feel **secure** deserves your attention now.

So, let this first Full Moon of the year become your **emotional wellness oasis**. Take this opportunity to **recharge** your soul, release anything that no longer serves you, and step into 2025 feeling emotionally strong and renewed!

AFFIRMATION
FULL MOON IN CANCER

"I HONOUR MY EMOTIONS WITH SELF-COMPASSION
AND CREATE SPACE FOR REST AND
NOURISHMENT."

FULL MOON
IN CANCER

EMOTIONAL HEALING

SELF-CARE

FAMILY

Gemstone:
Moonstone – Supports emotional balance and healing. Wear it during the Full Moon to release emotional blockages

Scents:
Jasmine, Lavender – These soothing scents promote self-care and emotional healing

Element: Water

ACTIVITIES
FOR THE NEXT 2 WEEKS

- Spend time with loved ones who provide you with emotional security.
- Go to the cinema, cook yourself something delicious, take a relaxing bath, and prioritize your well-being.
- Don't take anything too personally—your loved ones are probably just well-meaning.
- Call relatives or friends you haven't spoken to in a while—the call is long overdue!

FUN FACT

Our first Full Moon in January is called the **Wolf Moon**, a name attributed by the Algonquin people, Indigenous communities primarily from the region that is now Eastern Canada. The name comes from the hungry wolves crying on cold winter nights. (See! You're allowed to cry, too.) Symbolically, it represents strength and perseverance through the cold, dark winter months. It's a time for returning home, self-reflection, and coming together as a pack.

JOURNALLING
FOR THE FULL MOON

REFLECTION QUESTIONS:

- What emotional needs have I neglected lately, and how can I better fulfil them?
- How do I feel in my home and in my relationships? Do they provide me with security and comfort?
- Are there unresolved emotional wounds from the past that are coming to the surface and need healing?
- In which areas of my life am I holding onto old patterns or fears rather than surrendering to the flow of change?
- Which family issues or relationships are weighing on me, and how can I create more clarity and healing?

JOURNAL QUESTIONS:

- What does "emotional security" mean to me, and how can I create it in my daily life?
- How can I give myself more space for self-care and healing in the coming weeks?
- What are my emotional boundaries?
- Which emotions do I want to release to make room for healing?
- How can I support myself more and treat myself with greater compassion, especially in challenging moments?

SPACE FOR YOUR ANSWERS:

RITUALS
FULL MOON IN CANCER

Release Ritual:
Write down the emotions or painful memories you wish to release. Safely burn the paper in a fireproof bowl, allowing the flames to transform these feelings into ash, symbolising your release and letting go.

Gratitude Ritual:
Write down the things you are grateful for. This can include your family, friends, or personal growth. Take a moment to pause and feel the gratitude deeply in your heart, allowing it to fill you with warmth and appreciation.

Letter to your Inner Child:
Take a moment to write a loving letter to your inner child, fostering emotional healing. Perhaps a situation or a clear memory comes to mind—mentally return to that moment and feel the emotions of your inner child. In your letter, meet them with understanding, comfort, and support. Be the person you needed in that moment. End the letter with a promise to yourself, something that shows care, love, and commitment to your well-being moving forward.

Smudging your Space:
Energetically cleanse your living space and/or rearrange it to promote well-being.

Heart-Chakra-Meditation:
Visualise a radiant green light in your heart area. Take a deep breath and invite the unconditional, infinite love of the universe to flow into you.

SPACE FOR RITUALS, THOUGHTS AND NOTES:

HIDDEN GEM: SMUDGING

Smudging is an ancient practice in many cultures. It is used for **energetic cleansing**, creating a **harmonious atmosphere**, and promoting **well-being**. Different smudging herbs have varying effects on us and our surroundings. You can use smudging for spiritual rituals, meditation, or simply to enhance the atmosphere of a room.

INSTRUCTIONS FOR ENERGETIC CLEANSING

1. Choose Your **Smudging Herb** and Obtain a Fireproof Bowl:
   - Sage: Has purifying properties and drives away negative energies
   - Palo Santo: Promotes positive energy while cleansing
   - Frankincense: Acts as a protective and clarifying agent
2. Set an **intention** for the cleansing and visualise the space being filled with **positive energy** as you proceed.
3. **Light** your smudging herb and allow it to burn briefly, then gently shake (don't blow) the flame out so that the herb is still glowing and **producing smoke**.
4. Slowly move through the room, fanning the smoke into every corner, window, and door to **dispel negative energies**. Trust your intuition on which areas may need more cleansing.
5. **Open the windows** to allow the smoke and negative energy to exit. End the process by speaking a short **affirmation** or by **thanking the universe**.

Tips
- Experiment with different smudging herbs: Everyone has different preferences, so find what works best for you.
- Create a peaceful atmosphere: Play soft music, tidy up, or light candles to create a calming environment.

HIDDEN GEM: VISION BOARD
A VISUAL MANIFESTATION OF YOUR DREAMS

A vision board is a visual collection of images, words, and symbols representing your goals, dreams, and desires. It helps you **focus on your intentions** and become aware of what you want to achieve in life. By keeping your visions in front of you, you manifest them in your **subconscious**, becoming more motivated to take the steps toward them.

Today, we check our phones multiple times a day. So why not use your vision board as your background? This way, you'll constantly be reminded of your goals, anchoring the image in your subconscious. When you're reminded daily, you'll also become more open to the opportunities and possibilities that come your way.

3 Steps to Create Your Vision Board Using an Online Creative Platform:

1. *Create a new design*: Go to a creative platform or app and search for "Phone Background," or create a custom design with dimensions that fit your phone screen. Select a collage or image grid template, or design the layout manually to suit your preferences.
2. *Add images and words*: Look for inspiring images online or in your photos, add quotes or words that reflect your goals. They don't have to match exactly what you want to achieve but should evoke the right feeling in you.
3. *Save and apply*: Save your design and set it as your phone's background— now you're ready to manifest your vision daily!

29.01.2025
AQUARIUS
NEW MOON

NEW MOON
IN AQUARIUS

The first New Moon of 2025 follows with a big bang in the **innovative** and **clever** sign of Aquarius!
The New Moon in Aquarius brings a breath of fresh air and plenty of **crazy ideas**. The kind where you might think, *"Can I really make this happen?"* – the answer is: **Absolutely, you can!**
Step out of your comfort zone and into the **adventure**! You've had four weeks to ease into the new year, and now it's time to hit the gas! This is the perfect time to start **innovative projects** and **think outside the box**. Let those ideas and visions flow freely before they fade away into thin air!

What does this New Moon bring?
This New Moon gives you the ultimate kickstart in terms of **freedom** and **innovation**. It's the perfect time to launch projects that excite you – and no, they don't have to be conventional. **Think big, think unconventional, and follow that joyful spark inside you.** Aquarius loves breaking boundaries and trying new things. This is your chance to **break free** from the daily grind and approach things in a completely new way.

Focus:
The New Moon in Aquarius is all about **freedom** and **independence**. What do you truly want in your life? How can you free yourself from burdens that are holding you back? It's about manifesting visions that not only make you smile but also leave you in awe – the kind of visions that really move you forward. **Think outside the box!**

So, grab your ideas and get ready for a fresh start! The New Moon in Aquarius is here to push you to create new things and take what you truly want. **2025? The real journey begins now!**

AFFIRMATION
NEW MOON IN AQUARIUS

"I OPEN MYSELF TO NEW VISIONS AND MANIFEST
INFINITE POSSIBILITIES AND FREEDOM."

♒

NEW MOON
IN AQUARIUS

◇ INNOVATION

○ COMMUNITY

△ FREEDOM

Gemstone:
Sodalite – Promotes logic, rationality, and helps to implement ideas with confidence

Scents:
Eucalyptus, Grapefruit – Refreshing scents that encourage innovation and clarity

Element: Air

DO'S & DONTS

✓ More is more! Don't be afraid of being "too much"! You are exactly right!

✓ Share your ideas with others! Don't be afraid of commitment – together we are stronger!

✗ Curling up, hiding in a cave, Netflix marathon - absolutely no retreat or isolation! Get out there!

✗ The excuse: "But we've always done it this way!"

ACTIVITIES FOR THE NEXT 4 WEEKS

- Brainstorm new ideas and projects that inspire you. Create a mind map!
- Spend time with like-minded people who share your visions.
- Avoid old thought patterns and open yourself to new perspectives.
- Do something you've never done before. Enter a beginner mode!

31

JOURNALLING
FOR THE NEW MOON

REFLECTION QUESTIONS:

- How has my perception of freedom evolved?
- What are my talents and strengths?
- How can I use my unique talents to change my life and surroundings positively?
- Where have I found creative solutions in the past that helped me overcome challenges?
- Which old thought patterns or beliefs are holding me back from living the freedom and independence I long for?

JOURNAL QUESTIONS:

- What does innovation and freedom mean to me?
- How can I bring more freedom and independence into my life?
- Who is my role model, and why?
- What steps can I take to strengthen my independence and be less influenced by external expectations?
- Which relationships or connections in my life support my need for freedom, and which could be hindering my growth?

RITUALS
NEW MOON IN AQUARIUS

Gratitude Ritual: Write down what you are grateful for in terms of your freedom and independence.

Manifestation Ritual: Write down your most innovative ideas and visions. Imagine that you have already brought them to life. Visualise the freedom you experience through these new paths and hold on to that feeling.

Manifestation Task: Create a vision board for the year 2025 for a better visualisation of your innovative ideas.

Third-Eye-Chakra-Meditation: Visualise a radiant indigo light in your third eye, awakening your intuition and creativity. Allow yourself to recognise new possibilities.

SPACE FOR RITUALS, THOUGHTS AND NOTES:

12.02.2025
LEO
FULL MOON

FULL MOON
IN LEO

DATE: 12.02.2025

With a lion's roar, the next Full Moon arrives, bringing a **powerful** surge of **courage**, **confidence**, and a little bit of **drama**. When the Full Moon shines in Leo, it's time to send your inner celebrity back on stage and make yourself shine in the spotlight.

Say "No" to self-criticism: Sometimes, we are our own harshest critics. Today, be your biggest fan and allow yourself to feel **proud** of what you've accomplished. Have you recently doubted whether your grand ideas were too far-fetched or unrealistic? Maybe people took the wind out of your sails because they didn't understand your vision immediately. Don't worry – now is the time to leave those doubts behind and return to yourself. Applaud yourself for the path you've taken so far, and **be proud**! Stop hiding and show the world how amazing you are!

Don't let others' criticism get to you: When someone gives you feedback, ask yourself, "Is this really constructive, or can I just ignore it?" **Lions don't get easily shaken**! But be careful – don't let it turn into ignorance or arrogance! Constructive criticism is always welcome and helps us grow! So, find role models: Look for people who inspire you and encourage you to live your authentic self.

What does this Full Moon bring?

The Leo Full Moon encourages you to be **brave**. It's about putting your **talents**, **skills**, and **creativity** out **into the world** without constantly worrying about what others think of you. Maybe you've tried something new, and not everyone cheered excitedly – that's okay! Now's the time to let go of self-doubt and do your thing!

Focus:

This Full Moon is all about **self-expression** and **creativity**. Dance in the moonlight (or at least in your living room), sing loudly in the shower (and imagine it's a concert), and **express yourself**! But be careful – don't let your lion's roar scare your loved ones. A strong will is great, but don't become bossy with others!

You're not here to hide – so get out there and show the world who you really are. **The stage is yours!**

AFFIRMATION
FULL MOON IN LEO

"I TRUST MY INNER STRENGTH AND LIVE MY
AUTHENTIC SELF WITH JOY AND PASSION."

FULL MOON
IN LEO

- CONFIDENCE
- CREATIVITY
- EXPRESSION

Gemstone:
Citrine – Boosts self-confidence, courage, and creative expression

Scents:
Cinnamon, Bergamot – Energizing fragrances that enhance self-confidence and foster creativity

Element: Fire

ACTIVITIES
FOR THE NEXT TWO WEEKS

- Use your creativity for painting or crafting, etc.
- Create a playlist with songs to sing along and dance to!
- Avoid self-criticism and allow yourself to be proud of yourself.
- Grab your tribe, go dancing, and celebrate!

FUN FACT

The February Full Moon, called the **Snow Moon**, derives its name from Native American traditions, reflecting the heavy snowfalls typical during this time. Like the blanket of snow that covers everything and makes it appear new, this full moon offers us the chance to release what we no longer wish to be and step forward in our true essence—you are invited to rediscover yourself, sparkle, and shine like snowflakes.

JOURNALLING
FOR THE FULL MOON

REFLECTION QUESTIONS:

- Where have I recently found the courage to show up authentically and clearly express my opinions?
- What creative projects or ideas have I brought to life during this time, and how have they inspired me?
- What fears or self-doubts have I overcome to follow my heart and make bold decisions?
- How has my self-confidence evolved in recent weeks, and how can I maintain this positive feeling in my daily life?
- What have I learned about my inner strength and confidence?

JOURNAL QUESTIONS:

- What does courage mean to me?
- Where can I show up more and share my talents with the world without fear of criticism or rejection?
- Which areas of my life require more courage and authentic self-expression, and how can I strengthen these qualities?
- What creative projects or dreams lie dormant within me, and what steps can I take to bring them to life?
- How can I celebrate and appreciate myself more for what I've achieved recently?
- Where can I show up more and share my talents with the world without fear of criticism or rejection?

SPACE FOR YOUR ANSWERS:

RITUALS
FULL MOON IN LEO

Release Ritual: Write down all the self-doubts holding you back. Burn the paper to symbolically release these doubts and make space for your true self.

Gratitude Ritual: Write down at least three of the strengths or talents you are grateful for. Read them out loud and celebrate them.

Express yourself: Engage with a creative medium (painting, writing, music) without worrying about perfection.

Step onto your inner stage: Play your favourite song, dim the lights, and dance wild & free!

Solar-Plexus-Chakra-Meditation: Imagine a radiant yellow light in the area of your solar plexus. With every breath, your inner strength and self-confidence grow stronger.

SPACE FOR RITUALS, THOUGHTS AND NOTES:

28.02.2025
PISCES
NEW MOON

NEW MOON
IN PISCES

Welcome to the magical Delulu-Land – the place where your wildest dreams and fantasies can become reality! This New Moon invites you to softly dive into your **inner, spiritual world**, trust your **intuition**, and allow yourself to create your **wildest dreams**. With the New Moon in Pisces, you're entering a time when everything feels like a **dream**. It's as if you're stepping through a magical portal into a world of **fantasy** and **spirituality** – go with the flow! Pisces loves to dive deep into their **emotions** and **dreams**, and this New Moon helps you unleash your magic!

What does this New Moon bring?
Float on Cloud 9, and don't stay grounded – it's time to shape your **inner visions** and bring them to reality. You don't need to understand everything; **you just need to feel it**. With its **deep empathy**, Pisces connects straight to the universe through its **intuition**. Your feelings are the direct connection to your **highest self**, **deepest desires**, and longed-for **future**. The Pisces New Moon gives you that extra push.

Focus:
The Pisces New Moon is perfect for connecting with your **spiritual guiding team**. Meditate, visualise, and let your imagination flow – your dreams are the compass! This is about **creative projects, spiritual practices**, and a big dose of **trust in the unknown**. Don't worry about how everything works. **Just trust the flow**.

Here's your magical invitation to let your soul take the wheel! Delulu-Land isn't crazy. It's the place where everything is possible.

AFFIRMATION
NEW MOON IN PISCES

"I TRUST MY INTUITION AND MANIFEST MY
WILDEST DREAMS."

NEW MOON
IN PISCES

SPIRITUALITY

DREAMS

INTUITION

Gemstone:
Amethyst – Enhances intuition, inner peace, and spiritual awareness

Scents:
Lavender, Sandalwood – Calming fragrances that promote spirituality

Element: Water

DOS AND DONTS

✓ Daydreaming – Float happily on cloud nine!

✓ Sensitivity is your strength.

✓ Silence can bring you closer to your inner world.

✗ Don't let others influence you. Trust yourself!

✗ Make sure you don't become too sentimental in all your daydreaming.

✗ Be cautious of recklessness and its consequences.

ACTIVITIES FOR THE NEXT 4 WEEKS

- Meditate, practice yoga, and connect with your inner world.
- Spend time in nature, especially near water, to find clarity.
- Avoid haste and allow yourself moments of silence and reflection.
- Get creative with your hands. Paint intuitively without guidelines or work with clay.
- Create powerful affirmation cards! Repeat them daily to elevate your vibrations.

JOURNALLING
FOR THE NEW MOON

REFLECTION QUESTIONS

- What spiritual experiences have I had recently?
- What have I learned about my emotional needs?
- Where have I trusted my intuition in the past, and how has it guided me? How does my gut feel?
- What dreams and inner visions are particularly meaningful to me, and what can I learn from them?
- What have I dreamed recently, and have any patterns repeated themselves?

JOURNAL QUESTIONS

- What is the difference between head, heart, and gut decisions for me?
- How can I connect more with my intuition?
- What is preventing me from manifesting my dreams?
- What creative or spiritual practices help me strengthen my emotional and spiritual health?
- How do I envision the universe, God, or a higher power?

RITUALS
NEW MOON IN PISCES

Gratitude Ritual: Write down what you are grateful for in your life. Perhaps you are grateful for spiritual experiences or insights.

Manifestation Ritual: Write down your deepest dreams and visions. Visualise how they have already become a reality. Imagine the feelings you experience when your dreams come true, and hold onto those emotions.

Manifestation Task: Write a letter to yourself! Imagine yourself in the future (1, 2, or 5 years from now) and describe your life, your work, where and how you live, who is in your life, what you're doing, and how you feel. Describe everything that matters to you and explain to yourself what your life looks like. This letter can help with your manifestations and serve as guidance for your goals. Date the letter with a future date, and set a reminder for that day to read it again.

Crown-Chakra-Meditation: Imagine a radiant purple or white light emanating from the top of your head, connecting you to the universe. Feel how you become one with it!

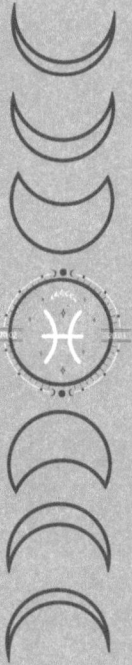

SPACE FOR RITUALS, THOUGHTS AND NOTES:

HIDDEN GEM: AFFIRMATIONS
WHAT ARE THEY AND WHAT DO THEY DO?

Affirmations are **positive, powerful statements** that help **reprogram thoughts and inner beliefs**. Inner beliefs are deeply rooted in our positive and negative convictions about ourselves, others, and the world. They often develop in childhood through experiences, upbringing, or societal influences, and they unconsciously affect our thinking, feelings, and actions.

By regularly repeating the "new" beliefs or affirmations, you can **strengthen the subconscious**, build more **self-confidence**, and **positively influence your reality**. Repeated affirmations promote positive thinking, reduce self-doubt, and focus on desired goals. They help break negative patterns and support personal growth.

Formulate affirmations in the **present tense**, **positively** and **specifically** ("I am strong and confident" instead of "I will not doubt"). It is crucial that they feel **authentic** and that you genuinely believe them - only then can they be effective and support long-term changes.

Tip for creating your own affirmation cards:
Make them beautiful and personal, either online or by crafting creatively. Print them out at a local shop if needed, or write affirmations on small pieces of paper and stick them in places around the house where you often see them - such as on the fridge, mirror, or door. This way, the positive messages become part of your daily life, and you'll be reminded to focus on your goals and strengths.

HIDDEN GEM: ECLIPSE SEASON
ECLIPSE WHAT?

We've probably all heard 'It's Eclipse Season...' but that doesn't exactly shine a light on the conversation for all of us. 'Eclipse Season' is the period of the year when **lunar and solar eclipses** occur. This typically happens **twice a year** and lasts about two to three weeks. Eclipses usually **occur in pairs**: first, a lunar eclipse, followed by a solar eclipse.

The zodiac sign the Moon is in determines the themes of solar and lunar eclipses during the Full or New Moon.
A **solar eclipse** only occurs during the **New Moon**, signifying a **new beginning.**
And since a **lunar eclipse** only happens during the **Full Moon**, it usually signifies a **farewell** or **ending**.
The **various spiritual effects and shifts** can be felt **for up to six months**, with the energy being most intense during the eclipse.

Lunar and solar eclipses only occur during **Full or New Moons**, as they happen at the **lunar nodes**.

HIDDEN GEM: ECLIPSE SEASON
ECLIPSE WHAT?

These calculated nodes, the **North Node and South Node,** are the points where the Moon's orbit crosses the ecliptic. The ecliptic describes the Sun's apparent path across the sky as seen from Earth over the year. The proximity to the lunar nodes determines whether an eclipse can occur.

The position and activation of the lunar nodes are crucial for the occurrence and prediction of eclipses. Still, they also have a deeper meaning in astrology: The **North Node** represents our **growth, soul's tasks, and potential**, while the **South Node** is connected to **past experiences** and the **resolution of karmic issues**.

The lunar nodes form an **axis** between **two opposing zodiac signs**. These give clues as to which energies and **lessons** we, often in a **collective context**, are meant to experience and process during an Eclipse Season in order to evolve and experience healing. The entire cycle of the axes and lunar nodes repeats approximately every **18.5 months**. During this time, multiple eclipses occur in the respective signs, highlighting specific themes and energies. **The axis of the lunar nodes thus activates the key themes for the entire cycle of over 1.5 years.**

HIDDEN GEM: ECLIPSE SEASON
FORMATION AND TYPES

A **lunar eclipse** occurs during a **Full Moon** when the Earth is positioned between the Sun and the Moon, casting its shadow on the Moon.

There are the following types:
- *Total Lunar Eclipse*: The entire Moon is in the Earth's shadow and is often tinted red, resulting in a "Blood Moon."
- *Partial Lunar Eclipse*: Only a part of the Moon enters the Earth's shadow, so part of the Moon remains illuminated.
- *Penumbral Lunar Eclipse*: The Moon passes through only the Earth's outer shadow, causing a subtle darkening of the Moon.

A **solar eclipse** occurs during a **New Moon** when the Moon is positioned between the Earth and the Sun, blocking the view of the Sun.

There are also different types here:
- *Total Solar Eclipse*: The Moon completely covers the Sun, leaving only the solar corona, a bright, diffuse ring, visible. This is a stunning event that can only be seen in specific parts of the world.
- *Partial Solar Eclipse*: The Moon covers only a part of the Sun, leaving a "crescent" shape visible.
- *Annular Solar Eclipse*: The Moon is too far from the Earth to completely cover the Sun, leaving a bright ring or "fire ring" visible.

HIDDEN GEM: ECLIPSE SEASON
SPIRITUAL IMPACT AND EFFECT

Eclipses, both solar and lunar, are cosmic events that signify **sudden changes** and **upheavals** – fast and often unexpected ones. They symbolize the **end** of an old cycle and the **beginning** of a new one. Partnerships may end, careers may take a leap, or new relationships may begin – often in ways we didn't anticipate and with a sense of urgency. Whether these upheavals are perceived as **positive or negative**, they always have an intense impact. The energy of eclipses acts as a cosmic catalyst – it especially brings movement to stagnant situations, often leading to profound insights or revelations.

In spirituality, eclipses are often seen as **transformative events**. They offer the opportunity for reflection and the release of burdens. Generally, eclipses can help reveal hidden aspects of the self and initiate personal change. These two types of eclipses also carry different meanings in astrology. Since the lunar eclipse typically comes first, it brings closure to themes in your life, while the solar eclipse pushes you to embrace new paths.

Lunar Eclipse = Full Moon = Endings
Solar Eclipse = New Moon = New Beginnings

HIDDEN GEM: ECLIPSE SEASON
LUNAR ECLIPSE

During a lunar eclipse, a cosmic chain of **endings** takes place. The energies shake us awake, forcing us to **release old patterns** and make space for the new. We are given the opportunity to **end old cycles** and let go of what no longer serves us. The energy of a lunar eclipse acts like a cosmic mirror: it brings **unconscious issues** and **blocked emotions** to the surface, encouraging self-reflection and inner realignment.

On an individual level, lunar eclipses can intensify emotional and spiritual processes. Relationships may be tested, patterns broken, and old wounds revealed to make space for transformation. Often, things end for us, typically when we have either failed to make a decision ourselves or were unaware that something was no longer serving us positively.

On a collective level, lunar eclipses can cause societal upheavals and breakdowns. Hidden issues that have been lurking in the background come to the surface, often leading to profound insights or political movements.

Overall, the lunar eclipse can initially be shocking, but it leads to essential changes and, ultimately, emotional healing.

HIDDEN GEM: ECLIPSE SEASON
SOLAR ECLIPSE

The effects of a solar eclipse are felt both physically and energetically. Spiritually, solar eclipses symbolize **new beginnings** and profound changes. They represent moments of darkness and **introspection**, followed by new clarity and insights.

For the individual, it can be an intense time of reflection and transformation, during which **sudden insights** and a strong urge for change can arise. It often reveals **new possibilities** and invites us to let go of the old and embrace a fresh start. It pushes us onto new paths and opens up unexpected opportunities that we might not have initially considered.

On a societal level, solar eclipses release a collective energy that brings previously hidden possibilities for change to light and sparks discussions about transformation and renewal. They can influence the perception and focus of entire communities and often evoke a sense of urgency.

Overall, the energy of a solar eclipse can be frightening, but it can also lead to significant personal growth.

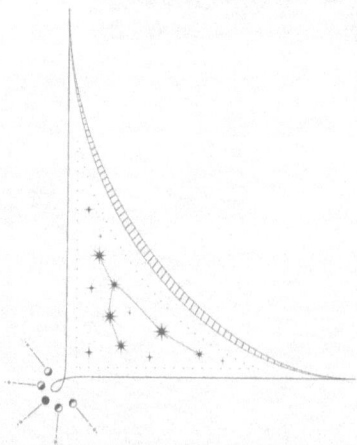

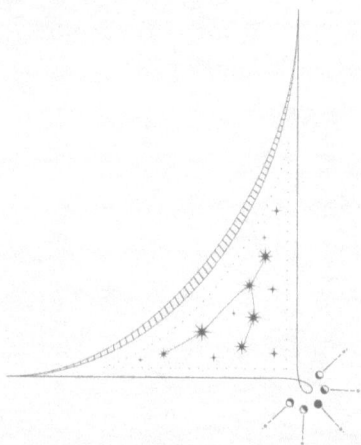

HIDDEN GEM: ECLIPSE SEASON

In summary, the Eclipse Season removes what is not meant to stay in your life. You may notice something falling away around the time of a lunar eclipse, while a solar eclipse could bring something new into your life. Overall, the Eclipse Season signifies a shift in our personal and collective energies.

The effects of eclipses can last up to six months, with the peak occurring in the immediate vicinity of the eclipse.

DONT DO IT!

Typically, a full moon is the perfect opportunity to charge your crystals in the moonlight. The full moon's light carries a powerful, cleansing energy that charges your crystals with positive vibrations. However, this rule does not apply during a lunar eclipse! Since the lunar eclipse represents change, instability, and transformation, you do not want to store this unstable energy in your crystals. **The energies during a lunar eclipse are intense and unpredictable - ideal for dissolving personal or collective issues, but definitely not something you would want to keep as a long-term "charge" in your crystals.**

HIDDEN GEM: ECLIPSE SEASON

There is also a widespread **myth** that **you should not consciously manifest during a solar eclipse**. However, manifestation is a continuous process that happens both consciously and unconsciously. The idea that we should not manifest during a solar eclipse is based on the assumption that the energies are "blocked." We are constantly working with solar and lunar energies during the new and full moon phases.

Although the light rays during a solar eclipse are indeed blocked, that does not mean the energies disappear. Instead, they are thrown back into the universe to return in another form. This can often lead to our wishes being fulfilled in ways we didn't expect. The universe's role is to realize these newly set intentions and manifestations in the best possible way. **While our manifestations during a solar eclipse can be wild and unpredictable, they are precisely the changes that help us move to the next level.**

Don't let the myths surrounding the solar eclipse hold you back. Trust the process because every solar eclipse offers a unique opportunity for new beginnings and personal growth. Use the transformative power of this cosmic event to manifest your desires and dive into your full potential. You are part of a greater whole, and the energy flowing during a solar eclipse and the universe are your allies on your path to your goals.

HIDDEN GEM: ECLIPSE SEASON
QUICK OVERVIEW

The cycle of the lunar nodes repeats every 18.5 months.

The key themes of this cycle are activated by the lunar nodes axis.

Axis = zodiac sign of the North Node + zodiac sign of the South Node during an eclipse

North Node = Soul's purpose, growth, potential

South Node = Karmic tasks and the dissolution of old patterns from past lives or experiences.

An eclipse always occurs during a full moon or new moon when the lunar nodes are activated.

The zodiac sign in which the moon is during the eclipse determines the themes the eclipse will bring.

Solar and lunar eclipses describe sudden changes and unforeseen events and symbolize the end of an old cycle and the beginning of a new one.

The spiritual effects of an eclipse can last up to 6 months.

Solar eclipse = New Moon = New beginnings

Lunar eclipse = Full Moon = Endings

HIDDEN GEM: ECLIPSE SEASON
OVERVIEW OF THE MAIN ASTROLOGICAL AXES

In astrology, there are several significant axes that represent specific themes and energies. Here are the most important axes summarized:

- **Aries-Libra-Axis:**
  - *Themes*: Individuation vs. Partnership
  - *Focus*: Balance between self-awareness and relationships

- **Taurus-Scorpio-Axis:**
  - *Themes*: Material security vs. Transformation
  - *Focus*: Dealing with possessions and emotional depth

- **Gemini-Sagittarius-Axis:**
  - *Themes*: Communication vs. Philosophy
  - *Focus*: Integration of individual experiences into a broader worldview

- **Cancer-Capricorn-Axis:**
  - *Themes*: Emotional security vs. Career ambitions
  - *Focus*: Conflict between family obligations and career

- **Leo-Aquarius-Axis:**
  - *Themes*: Creative expression vs. Collective thinking.
  - *Focus*: Balance between individuality and community

- **Virgo-Pisces-Axis:**
  - *Themes*: Practical applicability vs. Spirituality
  - *Focus*: Integration of spiritual insights into daily life

These axes represent the key areas of life where we experience tension and growth, balancing opposing yet complementary forces.

HIDDEN GEM: ECLIPSE SEASON
EVENTS OF THIS YEAR

Let's finally dive into the Eclipse Season of 2025!

Full Moon Eclipse in Virgo on March 14, 2025
Solar Eclipse in Aries on March 29, 2025
Full Moon Eclipse in Pisces on September 7, 2025
Solar Eclipse in Virgo on September 21, 2025

The eclipses will shift into the **Pisces-Virgo-Axis**, briefly returning to Aries (the **Aries-Libra-Axis**) in March. The last eclipse in the Pisces-Virgo-Axis will be a Full Moon Eclipse in Virgo in February 2027. Starting in 2026, we will also experience eclipses in Aquarius and Leo. Therefore, the primary themes that will influence us are those of the Pisces-Virgo-Axis and a short flashback of the Aries-Libra-Axis.

HIDDEN GEM: ECLIPSE SEASON
ARIES-LIBRA-AXIS

The Aries-Libra-Axis is one of the most important axes in astrology, as it addresses the balance between the **self** (Aries) and the **others** (Libra). It relates to the equilibrium between **individual independence** and **interpersonal harmony** and represents the ongoing balancing act between **self-realisation** and the pursuit of **relationships and cooperation**. This axis influences many areas of our lives, from personal goals and ambitions to our relationships with others.

The Aries-Libra-Axis has influenced us **since April 2023**, leading us through an intense cycle of **self-discovery, realignment, and partnership**. It has been about becoming aware of our own needs and goals. We have questioned our relationships and the balance between **closeness and independence**.

This axis's influence has been marked by strong polarisation: while the Aries aspect urged us to assert ourselves, **defend our independence**, and find our own identity, the Libra side repeatedly confronted us with the challenge of how we can **live harmoniously with others**.

During this time, we have repeatedly asked ourselves what is truly important to us in relationships. We have tried to find a balance—between the constant drive to please everyone and the feeling of being too selfish. We have learned to see **relationships as valuable additions to our lives** rather than as the foundation of our existence.

HIDDEN GEM: ECLIPSE SEASON
ARIES-LIBRA-AXIS

The Aries-Libra-Axis has urged us to seek **healthy relationships** – those that don't drive us into dependency but instead support us in living our true selves. Especially individuals with an anxious-avoidant attachment style or extreme need for independence have faced intense lessons, challenging them to trust, ask for help, and let people in. **Bonds have either strengthened or broken.**

So, what happens now, in March 2025?
The Aries-Libra-Axis will once again take centre stage, urging us to find a balance between **independence** and **closeness**. During this time, it will be about **final clarifications** and **decisions** in our relationships – what we are willing to give and what we need to feel truly fulfilled. We will again be challenged to find a balance that not only strengthens us in relationships but also helps us remain true to ourselves.

Overall, the zodiac signs **Aries** and **Libra** and **Cancer** and **Capricorn** will feel the greatest relief as we leave this axis behind, as these signs have most strongly felt its effects.

HIDDEN GEM: ECLIPSE SEASON
ARIES-LIBRA-AXIS

Around March 2025, this axis is likely to manifest in the following areas:

- **Self-Assertion vs. Harmony:** We may find ourselves torn between our own needs and those of others. The focus will be on how we can assert ourselves as individuals without jeopardizing our relationships. Conflicts could arise, prompting us to set clear boundaries or seek a solution that works for everyone involved.

- **New Partnerships and Changes in Existing Relationships:** March could be a time when we question old relationships and form new connections. It will be about recognizing where we have given too much and where it's time to bring more of ourselves into the picture. Relationships that are not aligned with our true needs may be tested.

- **Independence and Cooperation:** An intense energy of independence and striving for self-fulfilment will be present. At the same time, there could be a noticeable desire for cooperation and collaboration with others. The pressure to work as a team without giving up personal freedom may lead to tensions.

Overall, this period will offer us the opportunity to master the balance between individuality and community. The Aries-Libra-Axis challenges us to align our own desires with the needs of others and to develop a deeper understanding of ourselves and our interactions with others.

HIDDEN GEM: ECLIPSE SEASON
PISCES-VIRGO-AXIS

The Pisces-Virgo-Axis has been guiding us **since September 2024** and will remain active until the final lunar eclipse in Virgo in **February 2027**. Its impact is most strongly felt by the zodiac signs **Pisces, Virgo, Gemini, and Sagittarius**, as well as those with their ascendant in these signs. The main themes of this axis are:

Emotions and Balance
At its core, this cycle revolves around the balance between spirituality and reality. Pisces represents unity, intuition, and surrender, while Virgo symbolizes structure, order, and practical implementation. Together, they challenge us to translate emotional and intuitive insights into concrete actions and responsibilities. The Pisces-Virgo-Axis calls us to connect spirituality and daily life. It's not about losing ourselves in daydreams or abstract spiritual concepts but about putting these insights into practice. How can you use your intuition to make everyday decisions? How can your personal growth be translated into tangible steps? This axis teaches us that true growth happens when we not only feel spiritual insights but actively integrate them into our lives. It urges us to find the connection between visions and responsibilities and be equally present in both realms.

HIDDEN GEM: ECLIPSE SEASON
PISCES-VIRGO-AXIS

Relationships in the Make-or-Break
The upcoming 18.5 months will challenge relationships. Old connections may end while new ones form. The energy of the eclipses could urge you to let go of relationships that no longer serve you, encourage emotional openness, and allow vulnerability. People with Pisces or Virgo ascendants may experience intense changes during this time. However, the Pisces energy also offers the potential for deep, romantic connections and genuine soul peace.

Spiritual and Personal Growth
This axis emphasises themes of soul growth, consciousness expansion, and heart-centered connections. It calls us to find the balance between service to the collective (Virgo) and trust in the universe (Pisces). It's about embracing intuition and emotions while staying grounded in our duties and responsibilities.
- The South Node in Pisces urges us to let go, clear karma, and connect more deeply with spirituality and intuition.
- The North Node, activating Virgo, encourages us to focus on practicality, order, health, work, and growth.

HIDDEN GEM: ECLIPSE SEASON

Recommendations for the Eclipse Period

- Stay calm and relaxed. Trust in yourself and the universe. You will find and follow your path regardless.
- Observe your emotions with curiosity and openness—they might offer clues to themes that will periodically resurface until 2027.
- Use this phase to release old patterns and establish new, healthy structures in your life.
- Find ways to connect your spiritual growth with practical goals to create inner and outer balance. A great first step is having purchased this book! :)

The Pisces-Virgo-Axis wants us to embrace our vulnerability and find emotional clarity—a time to lead with the heart and act with the mind.

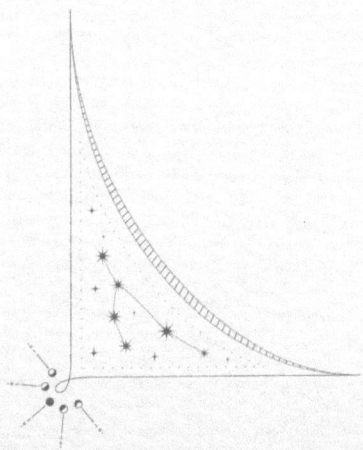

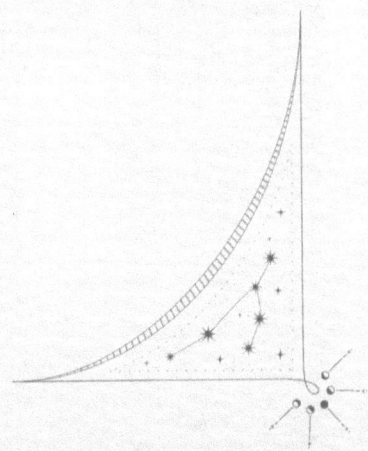

FULL MOON
IN VIRGO

Heads up, here comes the loop after the high-flying ride! The Virgo Full Moon tries to bring us back down to earth with both feet, but there's a bit of turbulence with the looming lunar eclipse!

True to the meticulous nature of Virgo, this phase brings a surge of **clarity**, **structure**, and a little "time for tidying up." However, there's a catch: the lunar eclipse is also in play, adding some mystical unease. What does that mean? Simple: It's time to pull out your to-do lists and check where your life could use a **spring cleaning**, but CAUTION—don't overdo it!

What does this full moon bring?

The Virgo full moon wants to help you **regain control over your life**. Anything that's fallen into chaos can now be **reorganised**. But be careful! Virgo tends to get too caught up in the details. We all know the drill: the desire to get everything perfect can lead us into the trap of **perfectionism**. If you get too absorbed in the minutiae, you might miss the bigger, more important things. Plus, the lunar eclipse adds a layer of confusion, throwing in a few surprises. Lucky for you, the universe will show you what you need to let go of - just relax, as it's probably beyond your control.

Focus:

The focus here is **self-discipline**, but the eclipse brings an element of surprise. This means you also get to lean back and accept that you don't need to have everything under control. Think about what you truly want to improve in your daily routine. What serves you? What drains your energy? Maybe you want to adopt healthier habits—better nutrition, more exercise—but also give yourself permission to delegate tasks and not have to handle everything alone. After all, we could all use a little help from time to time, right? **Don´t be a workaholic , please!**

Take breaks—it's okay not to have everything perfectly in hand. Your health and well-being should be a priority now, so don't stress. One thing's for sure: unexpected turns will come, so breathe through them and treat them as a fun challenge to improvise!

AFFIRMATION
FULL MOON IN VIRGO

"I CREATE ORDER AND BALANCE IN MY LIFE TO
PROMOTE PHYSICAL AND MENTAL WELL-BEING. I
FOCUS ONLY ON THE THINGS I CAN INFLUENCE."

FULL MOON
IN VIRGO

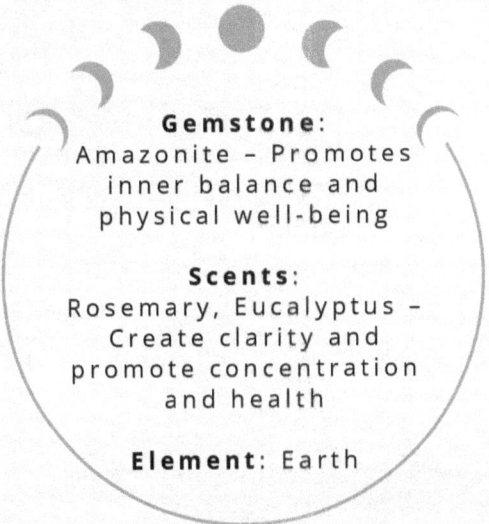

STRUCTURE

HEALTH

DETAILS

Gemstone:
Amazonite – Promotes inner balance and physical well-being

Scents:
Rosemary, Eucalyptus – Create clarity and promote concentration and health

Element: Earth

ACTIVITIES
FOR THE NEXT 2 WEEKS

- Revise your to-do lists.
- Do a spring clean and declutter thoroughly!
- Plan healthy meals and integrate exercise into your daily routine.
- Visit a spa or thermal baths for some relaxation.
- Delegate tasks and don't be a control freak!

FUN FACT

The full moon in March is called the **Worm Moon**, named by the Algonquin people after the first signs of spring when the earth thaws and earthworms come to the surface. This full moon symbolizes awakening and renewal. Just as the earth slowly awakens, this full moon offers us space for new growth. It's a time to set deep roots and prepare to start the spring with fresh energy.

JOURNALLING
FOR THE FULL MOON

REFLECTION QUESTIONS:

- How do I deal with loss of control?
- What have I done for my health?
- Which daily routines strengthen my physical, emotional, and mental health?
- What have I learned about the balance of body, mind, and daily life?
- What is preventing me from keeping promises to myself, sticking to routines, or consistently following through with new patterns?

JOURNAL QUESTIONS:

- What unhealthy patterns do I want to let go of?
- How can I better structure my daily life to promote health and well-being?
- How can I direct my energy and focus on what I can directly influence rather than being distracted by things outside my control?
- Which spiritual routines should become part of my daily life?

SPACE FOR YOUR ANSWERS:

Release ritual: Write down the unhealthy habits or patterns you want to let go of. Burn the paper to make space for healthy changes.

Gratitude ritual: Write down what you are grateful for in terms of your health and daily organisation. Thank yourself for your discipline and self-care.

Organisational ritual: Plan a week ahead by writing down your to-do lists and appointments to create clarity and structure in your life. By establishing this routine, it will also help you avoid being emotionally overwhelmed, allowing you to focus on what's important without overthinking each step, and keeping a clear mind.

Health Day: Dedicate a day to self-care – cook healthy meals, indulge in special body care, take a long walk, or treat yourself to a massage.

Root-Chakra-Meditation: Visualise a deep red light that grounds and stabilises you as you focus on your body and health. Give yourself stability and let the feeling of primal trust that everything is okay, as well as your self-confidence, support you.

SPACE FOR RITUALS. THOUGHTS AND NOTES:

29.03.2025
SOLAR ECLIPSE

ARIES
NEW MOON

NEW MOON
IN ARIES

The New Moon in March feels like a fireworks display! A golden shower of sparks kicks off with a loud bang: a solar eclipse! When the New Moon is in Aries, one thing is certain: **things are about to heat up**! Aries, known for its **fiery energy**, **courage**, and **fearless** approach to tackling the new, is the perfect companion when a solar eclipse comes into play.

This Aries New Moon brings you the opportunity to **ignite your inner rockets**. Have you been feeling a little slow or overthinking things lately? Don't worry – now's the time to take off! The Aries New Moon encourages you to act on your plans, charge forward with bravery, and risk it all. The motto is: **Full speed ahead!** But here's the twist: the solar eclipse will throw everything into a whirlwind. It may feel like being in a washing machine's spin cycle. Remember: this solar eclipse brings the themes of the **Aries-Libra-Axis** into the spotlight one last time, shining a light on the profound lessons of the past few years.

What does this New Moon bring?

Aries delivers incredible momentum but also a dash of **impatience**. If you've been toying with a project or idea for a while, this New Moon is the perfect time to finally take action. But beware: the solar eclipse might throw some unexpected obstacles your way. And guess what? That's a good thing! These surprises push you to think on your feet, test your **adaptability**, and discover new paths. With Aries fueling your fire, you're equipped to tackle any challenge. Trust that the universe has your best interests at heart, and try to spot the signs you may have overlooked amidst the chaos.

Focus:

This New Moon is all about **fresh starts, courage, and personal freedom**. The solar eclipse adds a layer of unpredictability, so stay open to changes and new perspectives. It's the perfect time to reflect on new goals, especially those tied to **independence, self-reliance**, and starting anew. Don't be discouraged if things don't work out immediately – the universe may have an even better plan for you.

Buckle up, embrace the surprises, and dare to charge ahead!
Don't let the solar eclipse dull your courage.

AFFIRMATION
NEW MOON IN ARIES

"I AM STRONG AND BRAVE, ENERGETIC AND FULL OF SELF-CONFIDENCE, I MAKE MY DREAMS COME TRUE."

NEW MOON
IN ARIES

- COURAGE
- KICKSTART
- CONFIDENCE

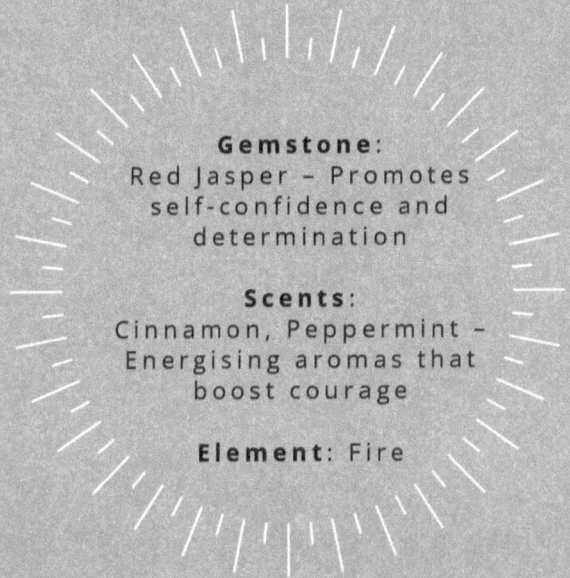

Gemstone:
Red Jasper – Promotes self-confidence and determination

Scents:
Cinnamon, Peppermint – Energising aromas that boost courage

Element: Fire

DOS AND DONTS

✓ Keep going and step on it!

✓ A new hobby, a fresh idea – just start something new!

✓ Go out and feel sexy! A hot flirt is waiting for you! You are on fire!

✗ Sit around and overthink.

✗ Give up when things don't go as planned.

✗ Be stubborn and selfish.

ACTIVITIES FOR THE NEXT 4 WEEKS

- Go to boxing, Muay Thai, or another combat sport where you can release your energy.
- Buy new lingerie to feel even better in your skin.
- Overcome a fear. You're full of courage and energy now, so leave one of your fears behind.

JOURNALLING
FOR THE NEW MOON

REFLECTION QUESTIONS:

- Where have I shown courage in the past?
- What have I learned about my determination?
- What successes do I want to manifest in my life?
- Which conflict between my individuality and independence and the needs of others do I want to resolve?
- What blocking and unhealthy behaviours do I want to leave behind?

JOURNAL QUESTIONS:

- What courageous steps do I want to manifest?
- What is preventing me from reaching my full potential?
- How can I strengthen my self-confidence?
- How would I describe my conflict resolution style?
- What does a "healthy relationship" mean to me?

RITUALS
NEW MOON IN ARIES

Gratitude ritual: Write down what you are grateful for in terms of your inner strength and courage.

Manifestation ritual: Write down your boldest goals and imagine achieving them with courage and determination. Visualise yourself mastering each challenge and confidently bringing your visions to life.

Manifestation task: Twist yourself into confidence, put on your sexy night-out outfit, and take yourself out on a date! Be bold and self-assured, feel sexy, and believe that you can have it all – because you can!

Solar-Plexus-Chakra-Meditation: Visualise a radiant yellow light in your solar plexus, filling you with energy and courage. Feel how this light spreads throughout your body, empowering and strengthening you. Let the warmth and brightness of this energy boost your self-confidence and determination.

SPACE FOR RITUALS, THOUGHTS AND NOTES:

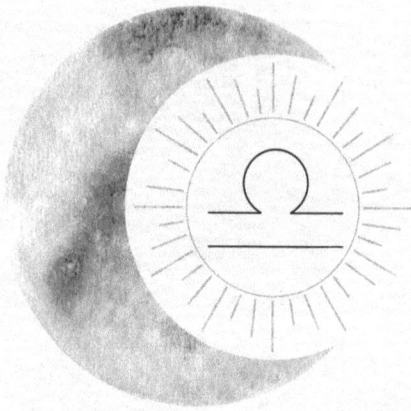

13.04.2025
LIBRA
FULL MOON

FULL MOON
IN LIBRA

Balance, balance, balance – after the intense eclipse season, this full moon helps us **return to our centre** and let go of anything within us that creates disharmony. It's time to reflect on whether, lately, you may have overwhelmed or neglected your loved ones in the heat of the moment. Now is the time to clear any conflicts or tensions that may have arisen and bring your **relationships** back into **balance**! We can finally invite **peace** and a few **loving feelings** into our lives.

The changing season is in the air. As the seasons shift so does the vibe: nature is transitioning, bringing new energy and a sense of renewal. This time encourages **growth**, **harmony**, and **balance**, inviting a sense of **peace** and **happiness** into our relationships.

What does this full moon bring?

The **charming** and **diplomatic** Libra encourages us to reassess and renew our **connections**. Consider which people bring you joy and which relationships may need some care. Perhaps some **friendships** need nurturing or extra attention—use this energy to **resolve conflicts** and openly communicate your needs. This is the perfect moment to clear up misunderstandings. Libra represents **harmony**, **balance**, and the art of **giving and receiving**. The Libra full moon asks you to pause and find equilibrium in your interactions. Where is it easy for you to give, and where do you struggle? How can you create more harmony? Take a moment to see things from the perspective of others. Make it your mission to ensure your loved ones feel loved and appreciated.

Focus:

Use this full moon to reassess your **values** and **priorities**. What's important to you? Are you living according to your values? What brings you joy and ease? Consider how you can give back the love you receive. Don't miss the opportunity to strengthen your connection with yourself and others. Spend time with people who inspire and support you, and **create moments of joy and light together**.

This full moon in Libra invites you to rekindle love—whether platonic or romantic—and move into the next season with fresh energy! Let the magic of Libra guide you and open your heart to new possibilities and deeper connections.

AFFIRMATION
FULL MOON IN LIBRA

"I CREATE BALANCE AND HARMONY IN MY
RELATIONSHIPS AND IN MY LIFE."

FULL MOON
IN LIBRA

RELATIONSHIPS

BALANCE

HARMONY

Gemstone:
Rose Quartz – Supports love, harmony and interpersonal relationships

Scents:
Rose, Ylang-Ylang – Promote harmony and love in relationships

Element: Air

ACTIVITIES
FOR THE NEXT 2 WEEKS

- Make someone a gift.
- Clear up misunderstandings in your relationships and look for solutions.
- Do a good deed and offer a favour every day.
- Give sincere compliments.

FUN FACT

The full moon in April is known as the **Pink Moon**, named after the early pink flowers, such as moss phlox (Phlox subulata), that bloom in spring across North America. This full moon symbolises the blossoming and fulfilment of new life. It is a time to nurture the ideas and visions we have planted and to pursue our future plans with confidence and optimism - ready to blossom and shine ourselves.

JOURNALLING
FOR THE FULL MOON

REFLECTION QUESTIONS:

- Where have I created harmony and balance in my relationships in the last few weeks?
- How have I improved my communication?
- What do I need to find more peace in my relationships?
- How do I give love, and how do I want to receive love?
- What are the love languages of the people I love?

JOURNAL QUESTIONS:

- What do I need from relationships to feel seen and valued?
- What does harmony mean to me?
- What should the ratio of give and take be? And how does an imbalance manifest itself for me?
- What conflicts occur in my relationships? What is the core conflict?

SPACE FOR YOUR ANSWERS:

RITUALS
FULL MOON IN LIBRA

Release ritual: Write down which unbalanced relationships or conflicts you want to let go of. Burn the paper to release these energies and make room for healthy relationships.

Gratitude ritual: Write down the relationships you are grateful for and why. Let this gratitude fill your heart.

Compromise Ritual: Write a list of conflicts or differences in your relationships and think of possible compromises to create harmony.

Core Values: Find your core values by writing down all the characteristics and values that come to mind. These can include honesty, freedom, growth, family, creativity, etc.
Use online lists of values for help and inspiration. Write down the top 10 that seem most important to you. Ask yourself: What things are non-negotiable for you? What motivates you? Think about different areas of life (work, relationships, leisure time).
Think about past decisions: Which decisions have you taken that made you proud? Which ones felt wrong? What motivated or disappointed you in those moments? You can also ask people who are close to you what values they associate with you. Now, gradually cross off the values from your list that seem less important to you than the rest until you are left with your top three. In the future, ask yourself whether all important decisions align with your three core values.

Heart-Chakra-Meditation: Imagine a pink light in your heart chakra expanding and bringing peace and love into all your relationships.

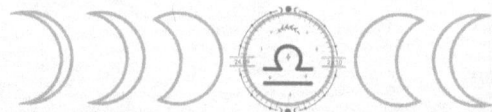

SPACE FOR RITUALS. THOUGHTS AND NOTES:

HIDDEN GEM: BELIEF SYSTEM
DON'T BELIEVE EVERYTHING YOU THINK

Inner beliefs are deeply rooted **convictions** we develop throughout our lives. They influence how we perceive the world, ourselves and our possibilities. They often arise in childhood, based on experiences, upbringing or social norms, and shape our thinking and behaviour.

Inner beliefs can be both **positive** and **negative**. Positive beliefs strengthen our self-confidence and ability to act, while negative beliefs can limit and block us.

Examples of positive beliefs are: "I am enough" or "I am funny." These beliefs promote our well-being and motivation. Negative beliefs such as "I am not good enough" or "success is only for others" can lead to fear, doubt and self-sabotage.

We often hear about inner beliefs related to personality traits or emotions – for example, "I am unlovable" or "I always have to be strong." However, these beliefs can be found **in all areas of life**, including topics such as money, success, and relationships.

A few examples:
- Career and success: "Only hard work leads to success." or "I'm not the type for leadership positions."
- Money and Finance: "Money is dirty." or "Rich people are selfish."
- Relationships: "I always have to adapt to be liked."
- Health: "I will never be fit." or "I can eat whatever I want."

HIDDEN GEM: BELIEF SYSTEM
DON'T BELIEVE EVERYTHING YOU THINK

Inner beliefs are important!
Inner beliefs are the **guidelines** and **filters** through which we see the world. They can motivate and strengthen us but also limit and block us. Positive beliefs such as "I can learn anything if I try hard" promote growth and self-confidence. Negative beliefs, on the other hand, can prevent us from reaching our potential - for example, if we believe we are not good enough to pursue our dreams.

By becoming aware of our limiting beliefs, we can check whether they still serve us and then **change them**. A negative belief like "I will never have enough money" can prevent us from recognizing or taking advantage of financial opportunities.

Inner beliefs shape our thoughts and actions. As soon as we consciously change them, we open ourselves up to new possibilities and can shape our lives more actively.
One effective method is cognitive restructuring, replacing negative thoughts with positive, empowering beliefs. Practices such as affirmations, meditation, or working with a coach or therapist can also help break old patterns and establish new, supportive beliefs. By consciously working on our thinking, we can redesign our reality and free ourselves from limiting beliefs. Here is an approach to transforming your inner beliefs:

HIDDEN GEM: BELIEF SYSTEM
6 STEPS FOR YOUR TRANSFORMATION

Step 1: **Raise awareness**
Identify inner beliefs that are holding you back.
- Write down what you believe about yourself, the world or particular situations.
- Ask yourself: "Where does this belief come from?" and "Does this belief serve me, or does it limit me?"

Step 2: **Question your Inner Belief**
Check whether the limiting belief is based on facts or is just an assumption.
- Ask yourself questions like:
  - "Who says that's true?"
  - "What's wrong with that?"
  - "How would I think without this belief?"

Step 3: **Understand the origin**
Find out where the inner belief comes from.
- Was it taught to you by family, society or experiences?
- Accept that this belief may have been helpful at some time but is no longer useful.

HIDDEN GEM: BELIEF SYSTEM
6 STEPS FOR YOUR TRANSFORMATION

Step 4: **Collect opposing evidence**
Gather examples that contradict the old belief.
- Write down experiences or moments in which the opposite was true.
- Ask yourself: "What new perspectives could I adopt?"

Step 5: **Transformation**
Formulate a positive alternative to your old belief.
- Make sure that the new sentence is realistic and believable for you.
- Example:
  - Old: "I am not lovable."
  - Goal: "I am lovable."
  - Alternative: "I have people in my life who love me."

Step 6: **Anchor the new belief**
Integrate the new belief into your daily life.
- Repeat it daily, e.g. as an affirmation.
- Act consciously according to this new belief.
- Visualize how you feel and what you will achieve if you live by it.
- Look for moments that confirm your new inner belief.

Tip: Be patient with yourself! The process requires time and practice until the new belief is deeply anchored.

27.04.2025
TAURUS
NEW MOON

NEW MOON
IN TAURUS

DATE: 27.04.2025

This month, embrace the positive side of the bull's nature: you are **focused**, **grounded**, and capable of achieving whatever you set your mind to. You may have been taking care of others recently and hopefully collected many **karma points** so that you can now look at what you want and need with a wave of powerful energy of **stability** and **grounding**!

The new moon in Taurus invites us to pause and reflect on our **principles** and **goals**, especially in relation to **material** and **financial** matters. Taurus is also full of **sensuality** and **enjoyment**. This means you can wish for the complete all-round feel-good package.

The new moon offers you the opportunity to **manifest the good in your life**. Have you ever thought about what financial or material goals you really want to achieve? Whether it's creating a **solid financial foundation** or investing in things that bring you joy, the Taurus New Moon encourages you to allow yourself what you deserve.

What does this new moon bring?

Taurus stands for **prosperity**, **stability** and the awareness of what we really need to feel **fulfilled**. What gives you a feeling of security and safety? Where can you bring more stability into your life? **Realign your goals and visions based on your values.** Use this new moon to strengthen your inner sense of prosperity. Allow yourself to enjoy pleasure and peace and embrace the finer things in life. **Life is too short not to enjoy it!**

Focus:

The theme of wealth includes **money**, **belongings** and **financial freedom**. In Taurus's practical and down-to-earth energy, this new moon asks you to **set a financial goal** or develop a plan to improve your material circumstances. Perhaps you want to set a **budget**, **invest** in new skills or increase your financial security.

Think about how you can use your financial resources wisely to live a life that brings you joy. It may be time to rethink old beliefs about money and possessions and make room for new perspectives.

Let this new moon in Taurus strengthen your intentions and open yourself to the abundance that life offers you.

AFFIRMATION
NEW MOON IN TAURUS

"I MANIFEST STABILITY AND PROSPERITY AND
ALLOW MYSELF TO ENJOY LIFE TO THE FULLEST."

NEW MOON
IN TAURUS

PROSPERITY

SECURITY

ENJOYMENT

Gemstone:
Emerald – Promotes prosperity and harmony

Scents:
Vanilla, Patchouli – Sensual scents that promote stability and enjoyment

Element: Earth

DOS AND DONTS

✓ Laze around. Enjoy the time off!

✓ When you buy, look for high-quality materials and durability.

✗ Stress yourself or let others stress you!

✗ Fast Food – Treat yourself to real food!

✗ Impulse buying and unnecessary shopping.

ACTIVITIES FOR THE NEXT 4 WEEKS:

- Treat yourself to something you have been denying yourself for a long time.
- Review your finances: Write down your income and expenses.
- Avoid unnecessary spending and focus on long-term stability.
- Treat yourself to a massage!
- Open a savings account to save or invest money.
- Dissolve inner beliefs about wealth and money!

JOURNALLING
FOR THE NEW MOON

REFLECTION QUESTIONS:

- Where have I created stability in my life in the past?
- What have I learned about my values and needs?
- Have I taken good care of myself?
- What do I think about rich people?
- What are my thoughts and feelings about making money?

JOURNAL QUESTIONS:

- What does prosperity mean to me?
- How can I bring more stability into my life?
- What does financial freedom mean to me?
- What do I dare to do? How much enjoyment and ease do I allow myself?
- What do I treat myself to far too rarely, and why?

RITUALS
NEW MOON IN TAURUS

Gratitude ritual: Write down what you are grateful for in your life, especially in terms of stability and security.

Manifestation ritual: Write down your financial and material goals. Visualise how you achieve these goals with ease and create stability and prosperity. Be precise: you can use numbers!

Manifestation task: Create a financial plan to achieve your long-term goals and put it into action. Set a savings goal and plan how much money you will put aside each month.

Root-Chakra-Meditation: Visualise a deep red light in your root chakra that gives you grounding and stability. Feel how this light connects you to the earth's energy and gives you security.

SPACE FOR RITUALS, THOUGHTS, AND NOTES:

_____
_____
_____
_____
_____
_____
_____
_____
_____
_____
_____
_____
_____
_____
_____
_____
_____
_____
_____
_____
_____
_____
_____

HIDDEN GEM: EMOTIONAL SPECTRUM
OUR FEELINGS AS SIGNS

Most of us learned early on to classify emotions as good and bad. However, the range of emotions is like a spectrum of colours - from bright, vibrant tones to dark, deep nuances. Just as bright colours only gain their radiance from dark ones, we can only experience positive feelings - joy, love, and satisfaction - in full intensity if we also know their opposite side: sadness, fear, and anger.

These "negative" feelings are not mistakes or flaws but necessary experiences that teach us the contrasts of life. They deepen our compassion, strengthen our resilience and give us the ability to perceive happiness and fulfilment even more consciously. Each of these feelings gives us clues about ourselves and our needs. They help us to promote our personal development. By dealing with them, we can grow and strengthen our relationships with ourselves and others.

1. **Fear**
   - *Indicates*: threat, uncertainty, risk
   - *Why it's important*: Fear protects us by making us exercise caution and **weigh up risks**. It shows us our limits and where we should be careful. Fear can also be a signal that we are trying something new and **leaving our comfort zone** - which often means **growth** and, in plain language: Do it anyway!

2. **Anger**
   - *Indicates:* injustice, hurt, frustration, or a feeling of powerlessness.
   - *Why it's important*: Anger shows that our **boundaries** have been crossed and motivates us to **stand up for our needs** or beliefs. It can be a **powerful driver** for change and help us assert ourselves rather than accept everything.

HIDDEN GEM: EMOTIONAL SPECTRUM
OUR FEELINGS AS SIGNS

3. Sadness
- *Indicates*: loss, disappointment, farewell
- *Why it is important*: Sadness shows us that something or someone is important to us and allows us to say goodbye and let go. It helps us process situations, **heal** emotional wounds and make room for new things. It also promotes **empathy** and strengthens our **resilience**.

4. Shame
- *Indicates*: A sense of failure, moral concerns, or a desire to live up to the expectations of others.
- *Why it's important*: Shame alerts us when we violate our **values** or **societal norms**. It encourages the need for self-reflection and can help us correct our behaviour or filter out **inner beliefs** that do not serve us.

5. Jealousy
- *Indicates:* insecurity, fear of loss or a feeling of lacking something.
- *Why it's important*: Jealousy shows us what's important to us and where we may feel **inadequate** or **insecure**. It also shows us if and where we're **lacking something**. It motivates us to work on our self-confidence and relationships by clarifying what we value and need.

6. Envy
- *Indicates*: comparing yourself to others, feeling like you don't have something you want.
- *Why it's important*: Envy reveals to us our **unfulfilled desires** and **goals**. If we use it as an **incentive**, we can be motivated to work in a similar direction and achieve our dreams instead of comparing ourselves.

12.05.2025
SCORPIO
FULL MOON

FULL MOON
IN SCORPIO

Are you ready to establish a **deeper connection** with both the universe and yourself? This full moon invites us to dive into our **emotions**, uncovering our **deepest feelings**, **secrets**, and **desires**. Its luminous glow illuminates our **shadow sides**, allowing us to embrace all aspects of ourselves.

Just like the **mysterious** Scorpio, this full moon encourages us to address hidden emotions and face the things we often prefer to keep buried. It's the perfect time to **heal old wounds** and step into personal transformation!

What does this full moon bring?
The full moon in Scorpio wants to help you make profound changes in your life. Scorpio is often associated with negative feelings, such as jealousy, mistrust or vindictiveness. However, it is a gift to have access to all of your emotions instead of repressing some of them into the depths of your psyche. Only when you fully acknowledge all of your emotions can you identify what might be holding you back from your dreams. **All feelings are valuable**, teach us and give us clues about ourselves and our path. **Powerful emotions lead to powerful events**. So use the powerful energy of Scorpio to dissolve old patterns, a relationship or even negative thoughts that are weighing you down. Scorpio helps us confront and embrace the darker aspects of ourselves, guiding us towards full **self-acceptance**. Make use of your wholeness and see all of your emotions as a superpower!

But be careful not to get caught up in an emotional spiral! Scorpio's transformative energy can tempt us to think obsessively about our feelings.

Focus:
Remind yourself that it's okay to **be vulnerable** and to **seek help when you need it**. Be willing to **feel your emotions** and draw strength from them. Scorpio energy promotes deep trust in yourself and others. Allow true intimacy and be surprised by what happens when you drop your mask. Often, the people we love already see us in our entirety and an even deeper connection simply takes place.

Your journey to **self-discovery** begins now: Let the **transformative** force of the Scorpio full moon initiate the changes you desire – and open yourself to a new, powerful version of yourself!

AFFIRMATION
FULL MOON IN SCORPIO

"I ACCEPT ALL MY PARTS AND ALLOW MYSELF TO
LIVE IN MY FULL POWER."

FULL MOON
IN SCORPIO

TRANSFORMATION

INTIMACY

POWER

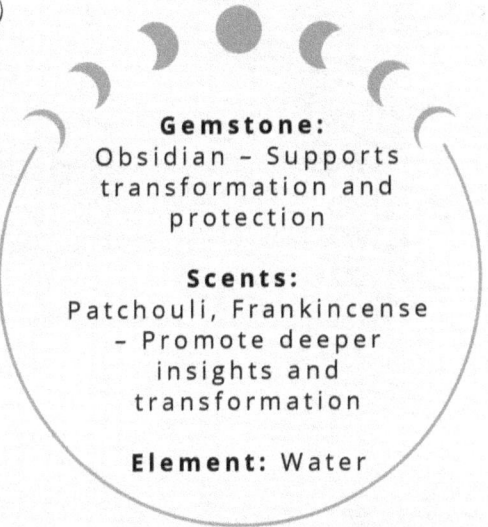

Gemstone:
Obsidian – Supports transformation and protection

Scents:
Patchouli, Frankincense – Promote deeper insights and transformation

Element: Water

ACTIVITIES
FOR THE NEXT 2 WEEKS

- Have a new spiritual experience, e.g. go to a new esoteric shop, do a tarot reading, go to a sound bath or see a new yoga teacher.
- Meditate!
- Avoid superficial conversations, share your deepest thoughts and feelings. Seek deeper connections.

FUN FACT

The full moon in May is called the **Flower Moon**, named for the abundance of flowers that bloom during this season in many parts of the world. Symbolically, this moon represents the awakening of nature and a time when our creativity can flourish. As flowers bloom and nature comes alive, we are encouraged to recognise and express our own inner beauty, talents, and passions. It is a time to open our hearts to the world around us, embracing growth and renewal in all aspects of life.

JOURNALLING
FOR THE FULL MOON

REFLECTION QUESTIONS:

- What changes have I undergone recently?
- How do I deal with power and control in my relationships?
- What have I learned about intimacy and trust?
- What emotions have been mainly present in my life lately?
- Which situations trigger strong emotions in me and why?

JOURNAL QUESTIONS:

- How do the following feelings feel in my body: envy, jealousy, anger, shame, love, fear, joy, gratitude and contentment?
- How can I give space to all my feelings without harming others?
- How can I deepen my relationships?
- What stops me from using my inner strength?
- Which emotions do I consider bad and what are their positive aspects?

SPACE FOR YOUR ANSWERS:

RITUALS
FULL MOON IN SCORPIO

Release ritual: Write down moments in which you felt powerless or power-hungry. Burn the paper to symbolically let go of these energies.

Gratitude ritual: Write down what you are grateful for in your life, especially in terms of transformation and growth.

Diary for emotions: Print out a yearly calendar or use the monthly/yearly view of your current calendar. Write down every day which of your emotions are predominant. Of course, you can also make further notes about the reasons. Feel free to write down everything to identify what is bothering you and then transform it.

Aura cleansing: Do a spiritual cleansing, such as a sea salt bath or an aura shower. Let all energies and negative traces go.

Crown-Chakra-Meditation: Imagine a radiant violet light gently entering the crown of your head from above, connecting you to the universe. You feel expansive and free as the light flows through your energy, giving you deep, transformative clarity about yourself.

SPACE FOR RITUALS, THOUGHTS, AND NOTES:

HIDDEN GEM: AURA SHOWER
CLEANSE YOUR AURA OF FOREIGN ENERGIES

Your aura is your **energetic protective cloak**. It is the energetic field that surrounds people or living beings and is often seen as an expression of **emotional, mental and spiritual states**. The aura shower helps you to free yourself from foreign energies that you accumulate every day and to **remove** negative **energies** and **blockages** from your own aura. This method combines water, which is a symbol of purification and renewal, with a conscious intention to promote energetic health. By concentrating on your inner balance in the shower, you can **leave the stress of the day behind** you and experience a feeling of freshness and lightness.

This simple aura shower practice can **easily be added to your regular care routine** and will help you relax, literally wash away negative energies and restore your **energetic balance**.

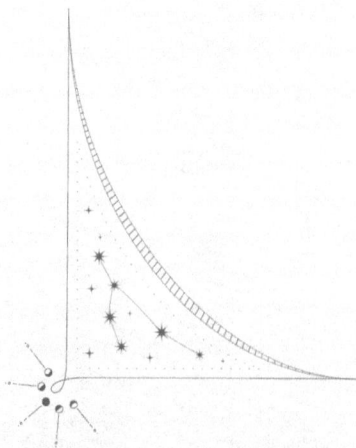

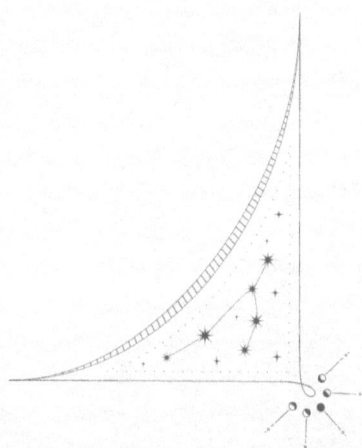

HIDDEN GEM: AURA SHOWER
STEP-BY-STEP INSTRUCTIONS

1. **Preparation**:
   - Prepare your shower and bathroom so that the room is comfortably warm and inviting.
   - You can also use soothing music or aromatic oils to enhance the atmosphere.

2. **Set your intention**:
   - Stand under the water and breathe deeply. Close your eyes and set a clear intention for the cleansing, e.g.: "I let go of all negative energies and feel refreshed and renewed." or "I let go of all energies that do not belong to me and feel liberated and light."

3. **Visualisation**:
   - Imagine that the water is like a beam of light washing away all the negative energies from your body. Visualise these energies flowing away with the water and disappearing down the drain.

4. **Breathing exercise**:
   - Breathe in and out deeply - just don't choke on the water. Take in positive energy with each inhalation and let go of everything that burdens you when you exhale. Focus on each of the 7 chakras one after the other and give each chakra a cleansing breathing sequence.

5. **Wrap-up**:
   - Finally, take a deep breath and end the exercise by imagining that your aura is clear and strengthened. After the shower, you can stand in front of a mirror and say and repeat a positive affirmation out loud. (e.g.: "I am relaxed, I am free and strong, I am full of positive energy.")

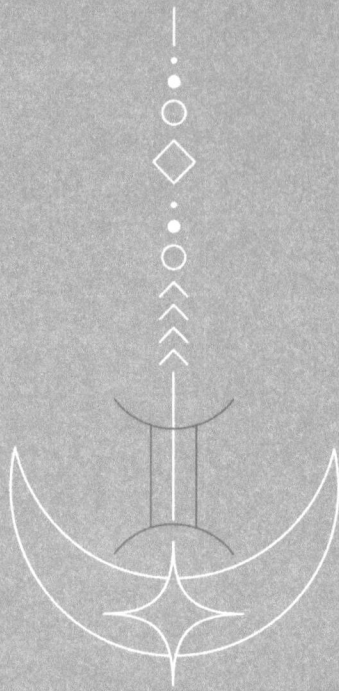

27.05.2025
GEMINI
NEW MOON

NEW MOON
IN GEMINI

The new moon in Gemini reminds us that **life is fun**! It brings a **refreshing**, **fast-paced energy** that invites you to get **creative** and improve your **communication skills**. It's the perfect time to start new projects that challenge your **speed of thinking** and get your ideas flowing!

What does this new moon bring?
You've spent enough time focused on your own challenges and worries. The **sociable** Gemini encourages you to go out and have fun! The moon gives you full **social batteries** or encourages you to recharge them with the people you love. **Be spontaneous and say "yes" more often!** The Gemini energy gives us **flexibility** and moments of laughter shared with friends. That's what we have this life for: to laugh, dance and have a good time in good company!

Focus:
The dynamic sign of Gemini encourages you to express your thoughts and ideas to the world. Maybe you have an **innovative** business idea, a creative project or just want to expand your social circle - the energy of this new moon will support you in this! Use this opportunity to build a network and improve communication with others.
Think about how you can **communicate** your messages clearly and effectively. What ideas do you want to share? Are there projects you've been wanting to implement for a long time? Gemini encourages us to be **curious**, ask questions and enter into **dialogue** with others.
But be careful, only share your ideas and wishes with people who mean well for you! The good nature and openness of Gemini energy can sometimes be exploited.

During this new moon, look out for **new opportunities** and possibilities. Let yourself be infected by the **fresh, dynamic energy** of Gemini and start full of vigour into the future of your dreams!
You have the power to turn your dreams into reality – so let's go!

AFFIRMATION
NEW MOON IN GEMINI

"I COMMUNICATE CLEARLY AND AUTHENTICALLY
AND ALLOW MYSELF TO EXPRESS MY IDEAS FREELY."

NEW MOON
IN GEMINI

- IDEAS
- COMMUNICATION
- FLEXIBILITY

Gemstone:
Garnet – Promotes grounding and determination

Scents:
Cedarwood, Sandalwood – Grounding scents that promote stability and clarity

Element: Air

DOS AND DONTS

✓ Party time! Whether it's a night at the club or a dinner with friends - the main thing is that you have fun and laugh until your stomach hurts!

✗ Don't take yourself too seriously!

✗ "Ghosting" has never been cool! Let us hear from you and get in touch with people close to your heart.

ACTIVITIES FOR THE NEXT 4 WEEKS:

- Start a new creative project or write down your ideas.
- Practice conscious communication and listen to others actively and attentively.
- Further your education, attend a seminar or go to a reading that interests you.
- Read a book or listen to a podcast!
- Go to a speaker event.
- Invite friends from different circles to a dinner.

JOURNALLING
FOR THE NEW MOON

REFLECTION QUESTIONS:

- What insights have I gained in the last few weeks?
- Do I communicate clearly and understandably? Are my messages received by the other person the way I mean them?
- What "figment of my imagination" keeps popping up in my mind?
- Which social networks, relationships and circles do I want to give more of my time and energy to?

JOURNAL QUESTIONS:

- Are there people around me who are experts in certain topics and can help me with a project?
- How can I improve my communication skills?
- Which conversations or projects need more clarity?
- What does fun mean to me?
- What was the last time I really laughed?

SPACE FOR YOUR ANSWERS

RITUALS
NEW MOON IN GEMINI

Gratitude ritual: Write down what you are grateful for in terms of communication and mental clarity, e.g. good conversations, inspiring ideas or new insights.

Manifestation ritual: Write down your most creative ideas and projects. Visualise yourself communicating these ideas clearly and effectively and making them a reality.

Manifestation task: Make a list of people or projects with whom you would like to express yourself more clearly and better. Also look for role models who are already living your dreams and visions. Learn about their life path! Maybe they have even written a biography.

Throat-Chakra-Meditation: Visualise a bright blue light in your throat chakra that helps you express yourself clearly and authentically. Imagine how this light strengthens your communication skills and helps you speak your truth.

SPACE FOR RITUALS, THOUGHTS, AND NOTES:

_____
_____
_____
_____
_____
_____
_____
_____
_____
_____
_____
_____
_____
_____
_____
_____
_____
_____
_____
_____
_____
_____
_____
_____

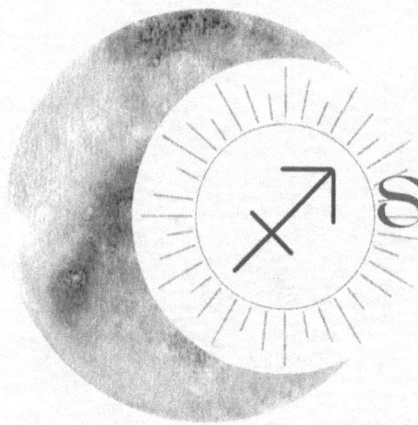

11.06.2025
SAGITTARIUS
FULL MOON

FULL MOON
IN SAGITTARIUS

Ready for the big leap? The full moon in Sagittarius is just around the corner! And it expects us to throw out everything that is holding us back from our next **adventure** and our sense of **freedom**!
It is the perfect time to **explore new horizons** and boldly follow your dreams!

The full moon in Sagittarius awakens a deep need for **personal growth** and **self-development**. Perhaps you have received new input, developed new ideas, exchanged ideas with others and your vision seems within reach. But something seems to be holding you back or making you smaller than you are? Perhaps you are wondering what really drives you, or perhaps everyday life has limited you a little recently. Whatever it is, today is the time to let go of exactly that! **Shoot like an arrow towards the future and share your light with the world.** Now is the moment to develop your full potential! Whether professionally, privately or spiritually - use the energy of Sagittarius and jump!

What does this full moon bring?
The Sagittarius full moon asks you to see **life as a journey** and to free yourself from your fear. Is there a vision that you have been putting off for a long time? Or perhaps a dream that you have not yet dared to pursue? Now is the time to think outside the box and look for ways to achieve your personal goals. True to the motto: Others have done it before!

Focus:
Listen to the crazy little voice inside you that always puts all those insane ideas into your head that you think are nuts, but whose ideas still make your stomach tingle. Listen to it as a guide to your wishes! It wants you to focus on your potential and make full use of it. It could be a good time to plan a trip, further your education or simply open your eyes to new possibilities that you may not have been aware of before.

Feel the spirit of adventure within you and use this powerful energy to push the boundaries of your comfort zone.

AFFIRMATION
FULL MOON IN SAGITTARIUS

"LIFE IS AN ADVENTURE AND I ALLOW MYSELF TO
LIVE IN MY FULL FREEDOM."

FULL MOON
IN SAGITTARIUS

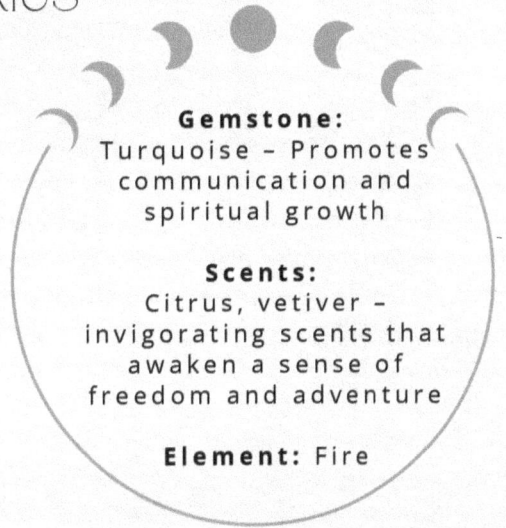

FREEDOM

ADVENTURE

GROWTH

Gemstone:
Turquoise – Promotes communication and spiritual growth

Scents:
Citrus, vetiver – invigorating scents that awaken a sense of freedom and adventure

Element: Fire

ACTIVITIES
FOR THE NEXT 2 WEEKS

- Remember that you have free will: eat cake for breakfast - who cares?
- Plan a weekend trip, journey or excursion.
- Do something crazy like: bungee jumping or skydiving!
- Fear is rarely a good advisor – instead, see it as an incentive for growth!

FUN FACT

The full moon in June is called the **Strawberry Moon**, named after the time when strawberries ripen in North America. This full moon symbolizes maturity, abundance, and harvest. It is a time to celebrate the fruits of our efforts. With gratitude and optimism, this moon represents the peak of spring energy.

JOURNALLING
FOR THE FULL MOON

REFLECTION QUESTIONS:

- What adventures have I experienced recently?
- What have I learned about my own limits?
- How can I bring more joy and freedom into my life?
- What have I always wanted to do but don't dare?
- Which countries have I already seen and which ones would I still like to visit?

JOURNAL QUESTIONS:

- Which cultures do I want to learn more about?
- What fears stop me from being brave?
- When was the last time I was really proud of myself?
- When was the last time I left my comfort zone?
- How can I broaden my perspective?

SPACE FOR YOUR ANSWERS:

RITUALS
FULL MOON IN SAGITTARIUS

Release ritual: Write down fears or limits that keep you from feeling free. Burn the paper to literally let them go up in smoke.

Gratitude ritual: Write down what you are grateful for in your life, especially travel, adventure, growth and courage.

Travel plans: Make plans for a future trip or a new adventure that appeals to you. Research the country, surroundings, culture and activities.

Stargazing: Spend time under the starry sky and reflect on your wishes and goals. Become aware of the vastness of the universe and recognize all its possibilities.

Sacral-Chakra-Meditation: Visualise a bright orange light in your sacral chakra, awakening creativity and joy. Allow the encouraging light to give you butterflies.

SPACE FOR RITUALS, THOUGHTS, AND NOTES:

25.06.2025
CANCER
NEW MOON

NEW MOON
IN CANCER

DATE: 25.06.2025

With the new moon in Cancer, we enter a phase of **security**, **healing** and **deep introspection**. After the full moon in Sagittarius encouraged us to let go of fears of the unknown and to dare new adventures, this new moon draws our **attention inwards**. It invites us to create a sense of **home** and **security** within ourselves - an **inner home that supports us**, no matter where life takes us and what challenges we face.
The essence of this new moon is to show you that **you already have everything you need within you!** It's about **self-care**, **emotional security** and the realization that "home" doesn't have to be a place, but also a feeling that we find and nurture within ourselves.

What does this new moon bring?
The Cancer New Moon is a perfect opportunity to connect with your inner sense of home. Take time to strengthen your **emotional base** and be able to support yourself: What does "home" mean to you? Is it a physical place, an emotional state, or the people who are important to you? How can you be a loving, comfortable place for yourself? Before you throw yourself into your next adventure, this New Moon asks you to manifest and create a **safe haven** within yourself.

Focus:
Direct your focus to the **connections with the people you love**. Cancer reminds us how important this **closeness** is to us. Because no matter how far away you may be, they remain connected to you energetically and emotionally. The Cancer New Moon therefore asks you to **nurture these relationships**, appreciate them and show your loved ones how important they are to you. Thank them for giving you a feeling of **love** and **comfort**!

Use the **gentle** and **sensitive** energy of this new moon to release emotional blockages and create security within yourself. Trust that the security you find within yourself now will be the foundation for all adventures to come.

AFFIRMATION
NEW MOON IN CANCER

"I ALLOW MYSELF TO MANIFEST EMOTIONAL
SAFETY AND HEALING INTO MY LIFE."

NEW MOON
IN CANCER

EMOTIONAL HEALING

HOME

COMFORT

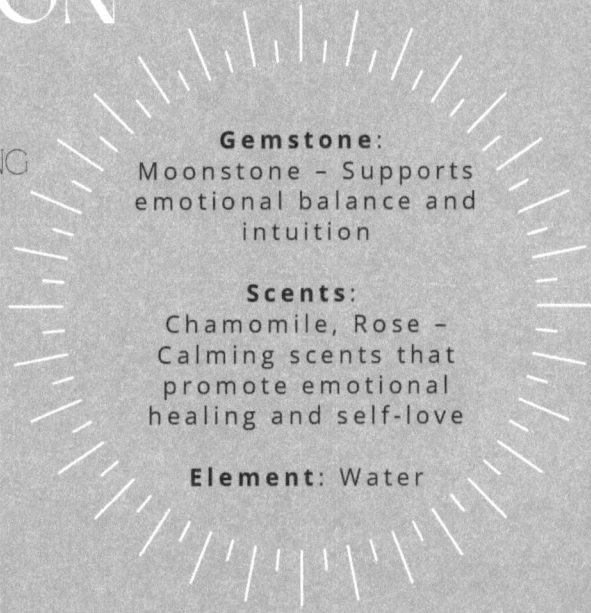

Gemstone:
Moonstone – Supports emotional balance and intuition

Scents:
Chamomile, Rose – Calming scents that promote emotional healing and self-love

Element: Water

DOS AND DONTS

✓ You can withdraw. Being alone is good for us.

✓ Everything that has to do with self-care.

✓ Express your love and affection!

✗ Don't be too sensitive and too critical of those around you.

✗ Fomo! You still have friends who want to do things with you, even after you've taken time for yourself.

ACTIVITIES FOR THE NEXT 4 WEEKS:

- Take yourself out to the movies or for a walk by a lake alone.
- Create a Pinterest board about your interior design or think about what your home should ideally look like.
- Renovate a room according to your ideas.
- Spend time with your family.
- Hug people who are important to you and seek physical contact (with their consent, of course).
- Throw a pajama party.

JOURNALLING
FOR THE NEW MOON

REFLECTION QUESTIONS:

- What gives me a feeling of security and stability?
- How did I advance my emotional healing?
- What family or emotional patterns have I identified?
- Where do I feel at home?
- Which connections in my life give me support and deserve more attention?

JOURNAL QUESTIONS:

- What emotional needs do I want to manifest?
- How can I better support and care for myself?
- How do "security" and "stability" manifest themselves in my behaviour?
- What does "home" mean to me?

RITUALS
NEW MOON IN CANCER

Gratitude ritual: Write down what you are grateful for in your emotional life and for the people close to your heart. Recognise the love and support you already receive.

Manifestation ritual: Manifest loving and healthy relationships as well as emotional security into your everyday life. Write down all the feelings that should fill your home and attract them into your life.

Manifestation task: Create a place of retreat, a kind of "shrine" in your home where you can regularly take time for yourself. A place that nourishes you emotionally and offers you security. This could be a meditation place, a cozy reading place or a place of relaxation. Decorate it with pictures, statues, gemstones and other things that make you feel good.

Heart-Chakra-Meditation: Visualise a bright green light in your heart chakra filling you with unconditional love and emotional healing. Imagine this light healing old wounds and giving you a sense of security.

SPACE FOR RITUALS, THOUGHTS, AND NOTES:

11.07.2025
CAPRICORN
FULL MOON

FULL MOON
IN CAPRICORN

Ready to take stock? The full moon in July is just around the corner and brings us the opportunity **to pause and refocus** in the middle of the year!

This full moon in Capricorn radiates a **powerful energy** that encourages us to take **responsibility** and bring **structure** into our lives. It is the perfect time to **refocus our inner compass** on our goals for this year, to rethink our **ambitions** and to become aware of where we are and where we want to go. Capricorn reminds us that success is not just a destination, but also a journey that requires **discipline** and **dedication**. And the full moon helps us to leave all previous stumbling blocks behind us in order to focus again on the path ahead.

What does this full moon bring?

The Capricorn full moon asks you to **appreciate your successes** so far while identifying the steps needed to realise your visions. It's time to not only dream, but also to **act**. What ambitions are really important to you? Where can you take on more responsibility? The full moon in Capricorn awakens inner ambition and the need for stability. Use this energy to **solidify your plans** and create a clear **roadmap for the second half of the year.**

Focus:

Maybe you made great progress in the first half of the year or there were challenges that held you back. Now is the time to leave everything behind and focus again on what you can still influence: **the future!** Gain **clarity** about your **goals** and use this powerful energy to work on your discipline. Ask yourself: **What can you do to get closer to your ideal self?**

Get out of the victim role, feel the responsibility you have for your own life and use this time to strengthen your foundation.

So, get ready to start the second half of the year with fresh energy. The full moon in Capricorn invites you to start afresh! **Realign your inner compass and strengthen your discipline - on to new heights!**

AFFIRMATION
FULL MOON IN CAPRICORN

"I TAKE RESPONSIBILITY FOR MY LIFE AND ACHIEVE
MY GOALS WITH DETERMINATION AND
DISCIPLINE."

FULL MOON
IN CAPRICORN

STRUCTURE

AMBITION

RESPONSIBILITY

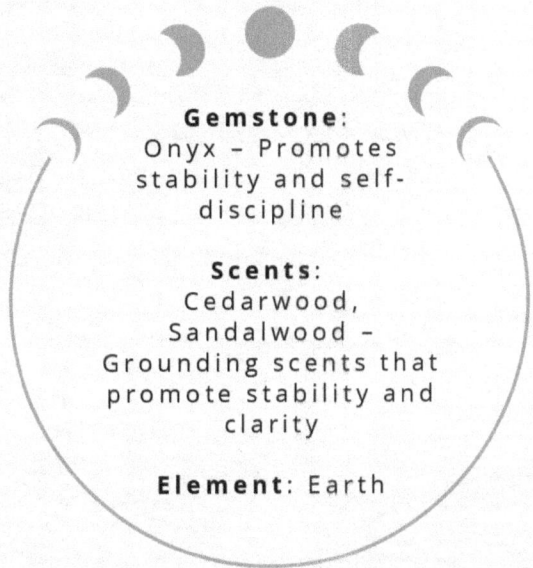

Gemstone: Onyx – Promotes stability and self-discipline

Scents: Cedarwood, Sandalwood – Grounding scents that promote stability and clarity

Element: Earth

ACTIVITIES
FOR THE NEXT 2 WEEKS

- Spend time in the garden or tending to your houseplants – potting or repotting new plants is a great way to connect with the earth and your surroundings.
- Take stock of your daily routine: Which habits bring you closer to your goals and which don't?

FUN FACT

The full moon in July is called the **Buck Moon**, named after the time when buck fully develop their antlers. This name originates from Native American tribes, particularly those from the northeastern and Great Lakes regions. The full moon symbolizes strength, growth, and reaching new heights. It is a time to pause and appreciate our personal progress and give thanks for all the experiences and challenges that have allowed us to grow. Be proud of your journey so far, celebrate your resilience, and look forward to the new goals and challenges that lie ahead.

JOURNALLING
FOR THE FULL MOON

REFLECTION QUESTIONS:

- What successes have I achieved in the last few months?
- How have I improved my discipline and structure?
- What is my inner demon telling me?
- What excuses do I make up for not doing something that I should actually do?
- What helps me to focus?

JOURNAL QUESTIONS:

- What goals do I want to achieve?
- How can I take more responsibility for my life?
- What stops me from being disciplined?
- What helps me to achieve inner peace and a state of concentration?
- Where do I find it easy and where do I find it difficult to take responsibility for my actions?

SPACE FOR YOUR ANSWERS:

Release ritual: Write down which limiting beliefs, habits or old patterns you want to let go of. Burn the paper as a sign of release.

Gratitude ritual: Write down what you are grateful for in your professional life, for which successes and structures you have achieved so far.

Set goals: It's halftime. Create an overview of your goals. Which ones have you achieved, which ones can you throw overboard or are done with, and of course what goals do you have for the next few months or years.

Action plan: Choose a habit you want to change or a goal you want to achieve. Create an action plan to effectively implement your dreams.

Root-Chakra-Meditation: Visualise a strong red light in your root chakra, which gives you stability and security.

SPACE FOR RITUALS. THOUGHTS. AND NOTES:

HIDDEN GEM: ACTION PLAN
A HELP TO PURSUE YOUR GOALS

1. **Definition of a goal:**
   - Formulate a clear and specific goal. What exactly do you want to achieve?
   - Example: „I want to run a half marathon."

2. **Analysis of the current situation:**
   - Consider your current conditions. What resources do you already have available? Where are you?
   - Example: Do you have a running partner? How many kilometers do you manage? Do you have running equipment?

3. **Identification of tasks:**
   - List all the necessary steps required to achieve your goal.
   - Example: "Register for a race," "Training to promote proper muscle development," "Go running three times a week."

4. **Allocation of responsibilities:**
   - Determine who is responsible for each task. There may be tasks that you would be better off handing over to experts or getting help with.
   - Example: Creating a training plan or finding the right running shoes.

5. **Challenges and conditions:**
   - Make the tasks you are responsible for as easy as possible. Eliminate potential stumbling blocks.
   - Example: Take your running gear with you to work so you can go running straight afterwards before the couch becomes more comfortable.

6. **Set a time frame:**
   - Set realistic deadlines for each task. This will help track progress and motivate you to reach the goal on time.

7. **Monitoring and adaptation:**
   - Schedule regular check-ins to measure progress and adjust the plan as needed if life gets in the way.

Stay positive and do your best! See the action plan as a tool to gain clarity.

HIDDEN GEM: SCENTS

Scents have an **extraordinary power**: they appeal to our senses, arouse emotions and can support us energetically. Essential oils extracted from plants contain the essence of the plant and their scents have a variety of effects on the body, mind and soul. Scents can **calm, stimulate, clarify or level**. Lavender, for example, promotes relaxation and inner peace, while citrus scents such as orange or lemon have a mood-enhancing effect.

They are particularly suitable for creating the right **atmosphere** in rituals or for **reinforcing intentions**.

So scents and oils are great companions for your moon rituals. Use them for meditation, as an anchor for an intention, as a supporting force when **cleansing a room**, or to **positively influence your mood**. You can use them in a diffuser or oil burner to fill the room with a suitable aroma, or mix oils like sage or cedar with water in a spray bottle to clear the energy of a room. If you put a few drops of diluted essential oil on your pulse points (e.g. wrists or behind the ears), the warmth of your body increases the diffusion of the scents, which can **directly influence emotions** and **well-being** via the limbic system. Our nose is directly connected to the limbic system in the brain - the centre for emotions and memories.

Therefore, scents can **harmonise our senses, fill us with new energy or give us a pleasant sense of calm**. They not only create an amenable atmosphere, but their chemical components actively influence our well-being. Scents help us to immerse ourselves in our rituals and **create a deeper connection to our inner world**.

24.07.2025

LEO
NEW MOON

NEW MOON
IN LEO

Clear the stage - here comes the appearance of the **creative** and **fiery** Leo new moon!
With this new moon we enter a spirited phase that offers you the opportunity to manifest your **self-expression** and develop your **creativity**. The lion, the sign of **courage** and **vitality**, invites you to appear **radiant** and **confident**. The new moon asks us to **polish our image** and look at ourselves through the eyes of others!

What does this new moon bring?
This new moon is your chance to look at yourself from the outside. How do you appear to others and is that the image you want to convey? **Adapt your outside to your inside.** Use this new moon to **manifest your ideal and best self**. It reminds you that you deserve to be seen and heard. The Leo energy shows us that there is nothing wrong with being the centre of attention, shining and being the hottest version of ourselves. So, **show yourself and be proud of who you are!**

Focus:
Now is the perfect moment to **start new projects** that are close to your heart or to revisit old ideas with fresh energy. Use this energy to make **bold decisions** and turn your visions into reality. Let inspiration guide you and don't be afraid to **take risks**. Allow yourself to let your creativity flow and **live your passion**. This new moon is the perfect opportunity to tackle the things that bring you joy and make you celebrate your uniqueness.

Get ready to ignite the creative fire within you and pursue your dreams with full force. Wear the flashy outfit or makeup, or don't wear it at all. **Be yourself and enjoy it!**

AFFIRMATION
NEW MOON IN LEO

"I ALLOW MYSELF TO SHOW THE WORLD ALL MY
FACETS AND TO FULLY DEVELOP MY CREATIVITY
AND SELF-CONFIDENCE."

♌

NEW MOON
IN LEO

CONFIDENCE

SELF-EXPRESSION

CREATIVITY

Gemstone:
Tiger Eye – Supports self-confidence and clarity.

Scents:
Orange, cinnamon – invigorating scents that promote creativity and courage.

Element: Fire

DOS AND DONTS

✓ Enjoy the limelight! You can be the centre of attention sometimes.

✗ All loud shouting and nothing behind it! Follow your words with actions!

✗ Don't be a diva! Self-confidence: Yes! But vanity stinks.

ACTIVITIES FOR THE NEXT 4 WEEKS:

- Do a photo shoot. Have beautiful pictures taken of yourself showing you at your best!
- Buy yourself a new outfit or a new perfume that makes you burst with self-confidence.
- Clean out your makeup and cosmetics drawer.
- Review your social media. Delete photos and posts that no longer represent you.

JOURNALLING
FOR THE NEW MOON

REFLECTION QUESTIONS:

- How have I expressed my creativity in the last few weeks?
- Which successes have strengthened my self-confidence?
- Where can I be more courageous and authentic?
- When do I find it easy to be the centre of attention?
- When and why is the opinion of others sometimes important to me?

JOURNAL QUESTIONS:

- What creative projects do I want to manifest?
- How can I further increase my self-confidence?
- What do I think when people are in focus and freely share their feelings?
- How can I counteract social anxiety?
- How can I express my personality through my appearance?

SPACE FOR YOUR ANSWERS:

_____
_____
_____
_____
_____
_____
_____
_____
_____
_____
_____
_____
_____
_____
_____
_____
_____
_____
_____
_____
_____

RITUALS
NEW MOON IN LEO

Gratitude ritual: Write down what you are grateful for in relation to your body, your creativity and your self-confidence, such as your talents, opportunities or successes.

Manifestation ritual: Close your eyes and imagine meeting your ideal, future self. Observe this version of yourself closely: What are they doing? What are they wearing? What energy and attitude do they exude? Pay attention to how they speak and interact with others. Write down everything that stands out: their hobbies, style, gestures, and interactions. Also, note how you feel as you observe them. Use these observations to clarify how your future self should live and act. Now, recognise that you are this person. Adopt these characteristics as your goals – and embody them until they become your reality! Fake it 'till you make it!

Manifestation task: Create a collage of images, photos, and quotes that represent your highest self and the vision you've outlined. Attach this collage to the inside cover of a notebook or journal, and protect it by covering it with a clear film. Each element should symbolize the qualities and aspirations you want to bring into your life, serving as a visual reminder of your goals and your ideal future self.

Solar-Plexus-Chakra-Meditation: Visualise a bright yellow light in your solar plexus that gives you confidence and inner strength. Imagine how this light awakens your creativity and gives you the courage to turn your visions into reality.

SPACE FOR RITUALS, THOUGHTS, AND NOTES:

09.08.2025
AQUARIUS
FULL MOON

FULL MOON
IN AQUARIUS

Change is often seen as something negative - perhaps because in the Stone Age, the tried and tested path actually ensured our survival and brought us safely back to the cave. But today there are no more saber-toothed tigers lurking when we take new paths. Keep in mind: change can scare other people because they have to re-categorise you and lose control of what is familiar.

But those who really love you will also celebrate the new version of you. The Aquarius full moon invites us to **courageously follow our own unique path**. It encourages us to **break away from social norms** and people who want to hold us back - and instead to **develop freely**.

What does this full moon bring?

Aquarius stands for **independence** and **revolution**. So you can let go of everything that limits you and makes you feel confined. The Aquarius full moon gives you the **space to think differently** and **find solutions that are unconventional and liberating**. Maybe you feel that it is time to question your position in society and in your environment. How can you reinvent yourself and give your individuality even more space? It's about questioning the norms and thinking about how you can have a **positive influence on your community** and the world.

Focus:

Use this full moon to **celebrate your uniqueness** and your inventiveness. Ask yourself: Where in your life do you feel like you need to dim your light? Are there areas where you feel like you are caught up in old patterns? Now is the time to break free from what is holding you back and to resolutely take new paths. Don't let the opinions of others sway you, instead, seek out your own **inner drive and motivation**.

Ready to break out of your usual routine? This full moon invites you to **write your own rules** and **follow your own unique path**. Feel the freedom that this full moon brings and allow yourself to act without fear of convention or the judgment of others.

AFFIRMATION
FULL MOON IN AQUARIUS

"I OPEN MYSELF TO INNOVATION AND FREEDOM
AND LIVE BY MY OWN RULES."

FULL MOON
IN AQUARIUS

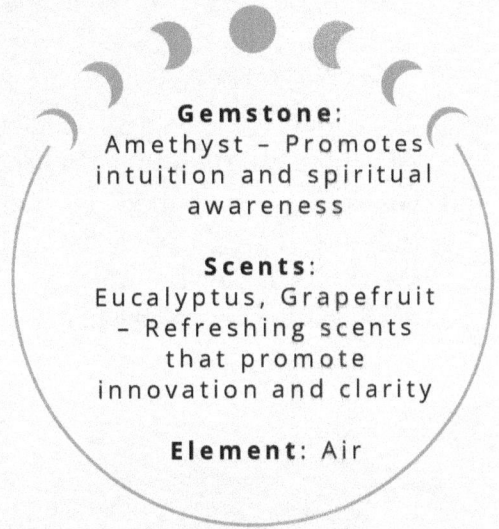

INNOVATION

FREEDOM

COMMUNITY

Gemstone: Amethyst – Promotes intuition and spiritual awareness

Scents: Eucalyptus, Grapefruit – Refreshing scents that promote innovation and clarity

Element: Air

ACTIVITIES
FOR THE NEXT 2 WEEKS

- Experiment with new technologies or ideas.
- Listen to an inspiring podcast!
- Do something with your family and friends that you have never done together before.
- Invite your besties and create together - paint glasses, jute bags or something similar.

FUN FACT

The August full moon, named by the Algonquin people as the **Sturgeon Moon**, invites us to pause and celebrate the results of our efforts. Like fishing for sturgeons, which require patience and perseverance, this moon reminds us that lasting success takes time. Use this phase to appreciate your progress so far and prepare for future challenges with calm and determination. Celebrate what you have achieved and trust that everything will come at the right time.

JOURNALLING
FOR THE FULL MOON

REFLECTION QUESTIONS:

- Where did I find creative solutions?
- What have I learned about freedom and independence?
- Which people support me unconditionally in my life?
- How often have I recently talked myself down or portrayed myself as better than I actually am?
- What was the last thing I did for the very first time?

JOURNAL QUESTIONS:

- Who do I admire in my environment for their uniqueness?
- What innovative ideas do I want to pursue?
- How can I express my independence?
- How would I describe myself?
- How would others describe me? Feel free to ask someone.

SPACE FOR YOUR ANSWERS:

RITUALS
FULL MOON IN AQUARIUS

Release ritual: Write down which traditional ways of thinking or old patterns you want to let go of. Burn the paper to make room for new ideas.

Gratitude ritual: Write down what you are grateful for in your environment, tribe, team or community.

Idea journal: Get yourself a small notebook and start an idea journal. In your idea journal you record spontaneous ideas, inspirations and creative ideas. It helps you to promote your creativity, organize thoughts and build a valuable bank of ideas. Everything that inspires you finds a place here, without judgment or limits. Regularly looking through and developing your notes makes the journal a valuable tool for implementing visions.

Nagging list: Negative attitudes as well as nagging or complaining cause our hippocampus, which is responsible for logical thinking and memory, to shrink. So do something good for your brain and keep a weekly tally. Every time you nag, criticise, complain or compare yourself, draw a line and take stock at the end of the week. Your goal is zero. Try to constantly improve. If you work out the causes, you can make long-term changes and counteract dissatisfaction.

Third-Eye-Chakra-Meditation:
Visualise a bright, indigo-blue light in your third eye, directly between your eyebrows. This light activates your intuition and inner wisdom. Feel how it gives you clarity to recognise new perspectives and find creative solutions.

SPACE FOR RITUALS, THOUGHTS, AND NOTES:

23.08.2025
VIRGO
NEW MOON

NEW MOON
IN VIRGO

Welcome to the world of **order** and **self-discipline** – New Moon in Virgo! With this new moon, we enter a phase of **clarity** and **structure** that invites us to improve our lives in **practical and sustainable ways**. Virgo, the sign of **precision** and **efficiency**, calls on us to become **mindful** and pay **attention to the small details** that often make the biggest difference. Imagine sorting your thoughts like a **well-organized** bookshelf and **laying the foundation for new, healthy habits**. With this new moon, we are laying the foundation for the next exciting eclipse weeks!

What does this new moon bring?
The effects of the **Virgo-Pisces-Axis** will intensify in the coming weeks, and this new moon gives us the chance to **prepare** ourselves for the challenges ahead. It is a call to **self-discipline** and to prepare for whatever lies ahead. The new moon reminds us that we should be mindful and respectful of ourselves. Because if we spoke to others the way we speak to ourselves, we might find that we would soon no longer have our social network. **It is time to lay the foundation for a loving and structured approach to ourselves.**

Focus:
This new moon asks you to examine your habits and your environment. Ask yourself: Where can I bring more structure into my life? What small, practical steps can I take to promote my physical and mental health? Now is the time not only to think about your goals, but also to **develop a clear plan for how to achieve them**. The Virgo new moon encourages you to **appreciate the essentials** and to give your life a **balanced structure**. Virgo energy encourages you to **pay attention to details** and appreciate the small changes that can bring big results in the long term. Whether you want to change your diet, exercise regularly, or structure your daily routine - the Virgo new moon gives you the push you need to consistently tackle these changes.

Get ready to establish new routines and organise your life with clarity and discipline. The New Moon in Virgo invites you to take practical steps to manifest your best self and to a healthier, organised future.

169

AFFIRMATION
NEW MOON IN VIRGO

"I ALLOW MYSELF TO MANIFEST HEALTHY
ROUTINES AND ORDER IN MY LIFE."

NEW MOON
IN VIRGO

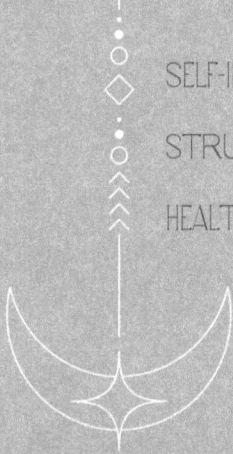

SELF-IMPROVEMENT

STRUCTURE

HEALTH

Gemstone:
Jade – Promotes harmony and self-care

Scents:
Lavender, rosemary – purifying scents that promote order and healing

Element: Earth

DOS AND DONTS

| ✓ Healthy meals, exercise and enough sleep! | ✗ Negative self-talk. Talk to yourself the way you talk to others. |
| ✓ Establish routines to make it harder to be lazy | ✗ Don't be too picky and critical overall. Take life easier! |

ACTIVITIES FOR THE NEXT 4 WEEKS:

- Go to your doctor for your annual check-up!
- Declutter your closets and organise your home.
- Try to have at least three positive experiences for every negative thought, encounter or statement!
- Organise to-do lists, write action plans - anything that helps you keep track!
- Donate clothes that are gathering dust in your closet.

JOURNALLING
TO THE NEW MOON

REFLECTION QUESTIONS:

- How have I supported my health in the last few weeks?
- Which organisational structures have proven successful in my life?
- Which routines do I want to improve further?
- Where have I been a perfectionist lately and gotten in my own way?
- How have I talked to myself lately?

JOURNAL QUESTIONS:

- What new routines do I want to manifest?
- How can I improve my health and self-discipline?
- Where can I submit assignments?
- In which areas am I particularly critical of myself?
- What routines can help me to be nicer to myself?

SPACE FOR YOUR ANSWERS:

_____

_____

_____

_____

_____

_____

_____

_____

_____

_____

_____

_____

_____

_____

_____

_____

_____

_____

RITUALS
NEW MOON IN VIRGO

Gratitude ritual: Write down what you are grateful for in terms of your health and self-discipline. Recognise the progress you have already made.

Manifestation ritual: Write down what new habits you want to integrate into your life in terms of health and order. Visualise how you effortlessly incorporate these routines into your everyday life and feel the positive changes in your life.

Manifestation task: Take a moment every day to compliment yourself. Whether it's about your appearance, your successes, your strength or your behaviour in certain situations - be honest and loving to yourself. At first it may be strange to praise yourself, but isn't it a shame that we so rarely give ourselves recognition? So, start your journey to a warm-hearted tone with yourself. You're great, so tell yourself that more often!

Throat-Chakra-Meditation: Visualise a bright, sky-blue light in your throat chakra that gives you clarity, self-confidence and the courage to communicate authentically. This light supports you in hearing yourself honestly and respectfully and in expressing your truth with confidence.

SPACE FOR RITUALS, THOUGHTS, AND NOTES:

07.09.2025
LUNAR ECLIPSE

PISCES
FULL MOON

FULL MOON
IN PISCES

The gates to the universe are wide open. Thanks to the full moon in Pisces, the path is more direct than ever before. We feel that the universe is listening. It feels as if our **subconscious** and our soul are **directly connected** to it - without detours. Use this opportunity to become one with the universe and fully **absorb the magic** within you! The full moon plunges us into a **mystical** phase that gives us **deep access to our intuition and spirituality**. Pisces, the sign of the **unconscious** and **limitless imagination**, gives us the opportunity to explore our inner worlds, to be guided by our **intuition** and to **dream** bigger than ever before.

What does this full moon bring?

The Pisces full moon invites you to **indulge** and **dream**. Let go of the pressure of everyday life and the weight of the earth and surrender. **Let your inner voice guide you**, because it is time to connect with your **intuition**. Especially in turbulent and stressful times, we tend to ignore our **gut feeling**. But this is precisely when it is invaluable. So use this full moon to pause, listen to yourself and give your inner voice enough attention. If you have perhaps tried to navigate your life rationally and logically in the last few weeks or months, then this full moon is asking you to let go and surrender to your emotions and visions. What is your intuition telling you? Where are you drawn to without being able to explain it? Now is the perfect moment to rely on and **trust your inner wisdom**.

Focus:

Use this powerful energy to look within yourself and find answers to questions that you may have been avoiding. The Pisces energy reminds you that it is often the **invisible, intuitive impulses that show us the right path.**

It is the ideal time to incorporate **meditation, journalling** or other **spiritual practices** into your daily routine that help you get in touch with your inner self. The Pisces full moon offers you the opportunity to explore the **emotional depths** and connect with **universal consciousness**. Let your dreams inspire you and realise that you are capable of manifesting great things if you surrender to the magic of the moment. Let go of all doubts - about yourself and the universe. Trust that the energy will guide you. If you are still hesitant, **let the universe itself convince you**!

Get ready to lift the veils between the real world and your dream world!

AFFIRMATION
FULL MOON IN PISCES

"I TRUST MY INTUITION AND OPEN MYSELF TO THE
WISDOM OF MY DREAMS."

FULL MOON
IN PISCES

INTUITION

DREAMS

SPIRITUALITY

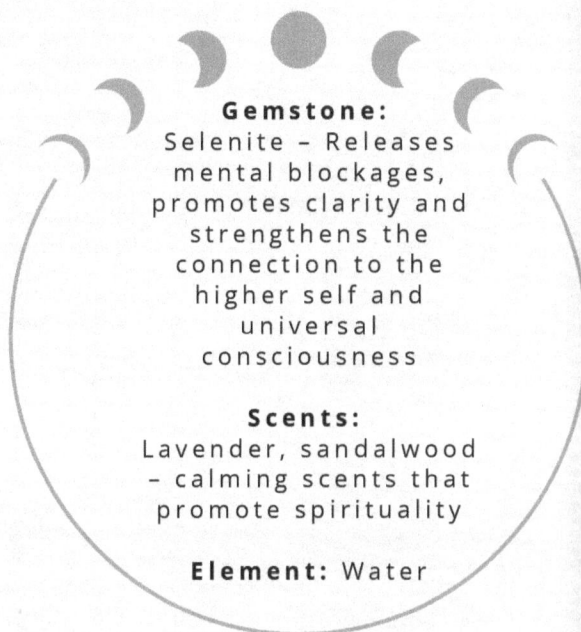

Gemstone:
Selenite – Releases
mental blockages,
promotes clarity and
strengthens the
connection to the
higher self and
universal
consciousness

Scents:
Lavender, sandalwood
– calming scents that
promote spirituality

Element: Water

ACTIVITIES
FOR THE NEXT 2 WEEKS

- Take time for self-reflection and meditation.
- Explore creative expressions that reflect your dreams.
- Avoid distractions and seek silence.
- Get tarot cards, a pendulum, oracle cards or another esoteric medium.

FUN FACT

The full moon in September, also called the **Harvest Moon**, marks the time of harvest, when the fruits of our labour are ripe. It is a time of gratitude in which we can reflect on the past year and celebrate our successes. This moon reminds us that it is important to appreciate the harvest time and to look back with joy and gratitude at what we have achieved.The name "**Harvest Moon**" originated from Native American tribes, who named it due to the close timing of the full moon to the autumnal equinox, allowing for extra light in the evenings to help with harvesting crops.

JOURNALLING
FOR THE FULL MOON

REFLECTION QUESTIONS:

- What insights have I gained from my dreams?
- How have I used my intuition lately?
- What do I need to deepen my spiritual connection?
- Which manifestations became reality?
- When did I feel supported by the universe and how did that manifest itself?

JOURNAL QUESTIONS:

- Which dreams and intuitions do I want to explore further?
- Which dreams and themes accompany me more often?
- Which emotions do I want to let go of to make room for new things?
- How can I strengthen trust?
- What was my craziest, most "supernatural" experience?

SPACE FOR YOUR ANSWERS:

YOUR TAROT
FULL MOON IN PISCES

Tarot cards don't predict the future exactly (unless you have a particularly well-trained tarot magician as a friend), but they do offer us valuable **insights into the moment** and **the energy that surrounds us**. The cards are more like **small, mystical mirrors** that encourage us to look **inside** ourselves and give us an **impulse** for our current situation.

To draw a tarot card, first close your eyes and breathe deeply. Let your thoughts calm down and concentrate on your intuition. **Let your question or concern arise inside you or say it out loud.** Tune into yourself and sense when the right moment has come to draw a card, and which one feels most aligned. Trust that the card you draw is exactly the one you need at that moment.

Before revealing the tarot card, take a moment to pause, breathe deeply, and tune into the feelings that arise within you. What sensations do you notice? Perhaps a pull, warmth, or sense of calm? These feelings may provide insightful guidance from your intuition, helping to reveal the answer to your question.

Once you have drawn the card, slowly open your eyes and look at it carefully.
Now formulate your **first impression** of the card: Which images, colours or symbols immediately catch your eye? How does the card feel when you look at it?

Write down the **main features** of the card and what it wants to tell you in the **context** of your question or concern. Pay attention to the meaning of the symbols and numbers and **reflect** on what its message means to you and how it **relates** to your current situation.

For more information, you can also research the card online and learn more about its meaning and symbols.

YOUR TAROT
FULL MOON IN PISCES

1.Question:
What should I let go of during this full moon?

1   2   3

2.Question: What should I embrace this full moon?

1   2   3

3.Question: Your message from the Universe

1   2   3

YOUR TAROT
FULL MOON IN PISCES

1. Question:
What should I let go of during this full moon?

1. XIV — TEMPERANCE

disharmony, inpatience, swerve into extremes

"I choose the middle path!"

2. XVI — THE TOWER

fear of change and the unknown

"I renew myself and grow.!"

3. IX — THE HERMIT

isolation, loneliness, endless seek for healing

"I am whole and carry the light within me."

2. Question: What should I embrace this full moon?

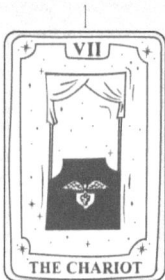

1. VII — THE CHARIOT

travel, confidence, success, determinatio n

"I choose who i am becoming."

2. XIX — THE SUN

joy, inspiration, love, abundance

"I am happy and radiate like the sun!"

3. VIII — THE STRENGTH

courage, influence, leadership, Anmut, inner strength

"I harness my inner strength for the greater good."

3. Question: Your message from the Universe

1. III — THE EMPRESS

Motherliness, love, wholeness, fertility, unity

"I take care of myself and create abundance!"

2. I — THE MAGICIAN

talent, resources magic, manifesta- tion

"I manifest my dream life!"

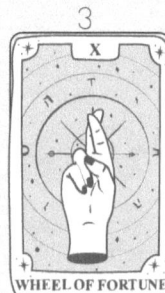

3. X — WHEEL OF FORTUNE

change, fate, karma, luck, flow of life, serendipity

"I surrender to the universe – everything falls into place!"

SPACE FOR YOUR ANSWERS:

RITUALS
FULL MOON IN PISCES

Release ritual: Write down what dreams or fears you want to let go of. Burn the paper to make room for new possibilities.

Gratitude ritual: Write down what you are grateful for in your spiritual life.

Dream Journal: Keep a dream diary in which you record your dreams.

Angel Meditation: Angel meditation is a powerful practice that connects you with your Spirit Guides. Begin by breathing calmly and relaxing. During meditation, ask for the names of the angels who guide you. The first names that come to mind—no matter how unusual or crazy they may seem—are the right ones. Trust your intuition to guide you and receive the names and messages of the angels offering you protection and support. This meditation can help you connect more deeply with your spiritual self and inner wisdom. After you receive the names of your angels, you can find out more about them by searching for information online. There are many resources that can provide you with deeper insight into the characteristics and messages of these angels.

Third-Eye-Chakra-Meditation:
Visualise a brilliant indigo-blue light expanding into your Third-Eye-Chakra, the centre of your intuition and wisdom. Feel this light creating clarity and insight in your mind. It helps you quiet the noise and distractions of the outside world so you can listen to your inner voice. Feel yourself connecting with your higher self.

SPACE FOR RITUALS, THOUGHTS, AND NOTES:

HIDDEN GEM: DREAM JOURNAL
A DEEP DIVE INTO YOUR SUBCONSCIOUS

A dream journal is a powerful tool for gaining deeper access to your subconscious. By regularly writing down your dreams, you create a valuable opportunity to engage with the symbols, feelings and messages your dreams convey. Frequently recurring themes or symbols can help you recognise patterns in your life, be it in your fears, desires or unresolved conflicts. This not only promotes self-reflection, but also awareness of areas where you may still have room to grow or heal.

What should you pay attention to?
Timing: Write down your dreams immediately after waking up. Memory often fades quickly, and the sooner you record the dream, the more detail you will remember.

Mindfulness: Pay attention not only to the plot, but also to the feelings, colours and impressions you had during the dream. These details are often crucial to understanding the true meaning.

Openness: Be open to what comes up without immediately judging or analysing it. Sometimes it takes time to decipher the deeper meanings.

A dream journal can not only help you better understand your dreams, but can also serve as a valuable tool for personal development and spiritual insight.

HIDDEN GEM: GEMSTONES

Gemstones have been known for their energetic effects for centuries and are often used in rituals and spiritual practices. Each stone carries its **own frequency** and supports us in different areas of life.

The energy of gemstones can help us **balance emotions, harmonise chakras or strengthen intentions**. They often serve as anchors in rituals to focus on a specific goal - such as **healing, protection** or **growth**.

In order for gemstones to retain and develop their effect, regular discharging and recharging is important:

- **Discharge**: Place the stones on a bowl of hematite or clean them with running water. This removes accumulated energies.
- **Charging**: Charge them under the morning sun, in the moonlight or on a rock crystal or amethyst cluster. Full moons are particularly ideal for supplying stones with fresh energy.

Gemstones can be used in many different ways in rituals and in everyday life. You can wear them on your body, hold them in your hand to feel their energetic effect, or place them on your vision board or "shrine" as support. In this way, you integrate the **powerful energy field** of the stones into your life and create a **harmonious connection** to their energy.

21.09.2025
SOLAR ECLIPSE

VIRGO
NEW MOON

NEW MOON
IN VIRGO

Let the grounded and down-to-earth Virgo energy calm you down! This New Moon is a reminder of the foundations we laid with the New Moon last month. It's about **resuming our routines and order**, and remembering that no matter how turbulent the times around us may be, **we have prepared well**. We are not only ready for external challenges, but also for the internal challenges that may arise during this intense time. Virgo supports us in making our dreams our reality with her **eye for detail**!

What does this new moon bring?

The New Moon in Virgo and the Solar Eclipse challenge us to find balance in both the physical and spiritual worlds. Virgo, the sign of **precision** and **efficiency**, invites us to incorporate practical changes into our lives that will help us reach our full potential. **It's about creating order - not only in our environment, but also within ourselves.**

The coming time calls for a conscious **harmony between our worldly life and our spiritual practices**. This cosmic energy calls us not only to be active in the material world, but also to make time for our inner growth. We should integrate spiritual practices that nourish our mind and soul into our daily routine and make them an integral part of our lives. Amid the changes and the incessant movement of life, it is all about staying in harmony with ourselves. We can focus on developing **healthy habits** over the next few weeks, focusing on what really matters: a balance between the practical aspects of life and our spiritual growth.

Focus:

The new moon and solar eclipse remind us that every path brings its challenges - whether it's choosing between feeling uncomfortable in your body or dragging yourself to the gym. **"Pick your hard!"** - Every decision comes with challenges. But it's up to you which path you choose. **Consciously choose the path of transformation and spiritual growth.** Know that you have the power to **make the best of both worlds** - and it's the perfect time to move forward with **intention**, **discipline**, and a **clear focus** on your goals.

You've got this! Trust in your inner strength and the universe! Virgo energy reminds us that we are constantly growing and improving!

AFFIRMATION
NEW MOON IN VIRGO

"I FIND BALANCE BETWEEN MY PHYSICAL AND SPIRITUAL WORLDS AND FACE EVERY CHALLENGE WITH CLARITY AND INTENTION. EVERY STEP BRINGS ME CLOSER TO MY TRUE SELF, AND I TRUST THE PROCESS OF GROWTH AND TRANSFORMATION. I AM PREPARED FOR WHATEVER COMES, BECAUSE I HAVE LAID THE FOUNDATION FOR SUCCESS AND WELL-BEING."

NEW MOON
IN VIRGO

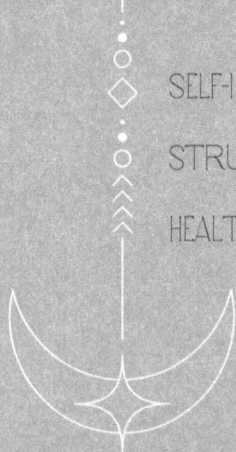

◇ SELF-IMPROVEMENT

○ STRUCTURE

HEALTH

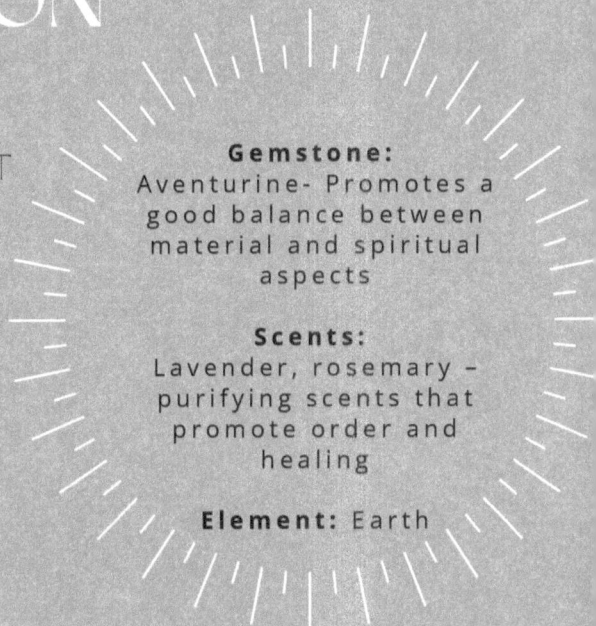

Gemstone:
Aventurine- Promotes a good balance between material and spiritual aspects

Scents:
Lavender, rosemary – purifying scents that promote order and healing

Element: Earth

DO'S AND DONTS

✓ Find balance and equilibrium in your life!

✓ Ground yourself. Foster your inner strength through calming practices.

✗ Criticism of everything! Try to see the positive.

✗ Control addiction! Let go of what you have no control over.

ACTIVITIES FOR THE NEXT 4 WEEKS:

- Go into the forest and collect natural materials and create a mandala.
- Get out your routines, to-do lists and action plans and keep going.
- Try Pilates.
- Meet up with a friend and empty drawers and clean your apartments together. Turn the music off and make it a "cleaning party" where you take turns helping each other.

JOURNALLING
FOR THE NEW MOON

REFLECTION QUESTIONS:

- What has changed in the last 4 weeks?
- Which routines and plans could I follow and which not?
- What obstacles arose and how did I deal with them?
- Which organisational structures have proven successful in my life?
- Which routines do I want to improve further?

JOURNAL QUESTIONS:

- How have I supported my health in the last few weeks?
- How can I better integrate my spiritual side into my everyday life?
- Do I feel more present on an earthly level or a spiritual level?
- How can I create a better balance and equilibrium for myself?
- What do I need to feel good overall?

RITUALS
NEW MOON IN VIRGO

Gratitude ritual: Write down what you are grateful for in terms of your health, your balance, and your earthly and spiritual successes. Recognise the small progress you have already made.

Manifestation Ritual: Manifest your goals related to health, wholeness, and balancing earthly and spiritual habits. Imagine these new routines fitting effortlessly into your daily structure and feel them creating positive changes in your life.

Manifestation task: Create new affirmation cards and integrate them into your daily routine! Repeat the affirmations daily.

Root-Chakra-Meditation: Visualise a bright red light in your root chakra that gives you trust and stability. Imagine how this light strengthens your health and helps you to manifest orderly structures in your life.

_____
_____
_____
_____
_____
_____
_____
_____
_____
_____
_____
_____
_____
_____
_____
_____
_____
_____
_____
_____
_____
_____
_____
_____
_____

07.10.2025
ARIES
FULL MOON

FULL MOON
IN ARIES

The storm is over! This fiery and powerful full moon is here to leave all your raging emotions behind you and give you courage for the rest of your journey!

Aries, known for its **fearless** and **impulsive** nature, gives you the drive to move past the turbulence of the past weeks. It encourages you to release emotional blockages and low frequencies, making room for fresh, new energy. Now is the perfect time to let go of emotional baggage and create space for new opportunities.

What does this full moon bring?

This full moon asks you to **free yourself** from the emotions that are holding you back and leave your past behind. Although Aries feels **intensely**, they never hold on for long and **quickly move on** to new challenges. Use this **bold energy** to find a moment of gratitude for all that you have accomplished. Gratitude opens your heart and allows you to see the good in your life. Perhaps you have made **brave** decisions or overcome challenges recently - take time to appreciate those accomplishments. Leave the past behind, be grateful for the lessons you have learned, and look to the future with **confidence**.

Focus:

The Aries full moon invites you to **rekindle your fire** and **recharge your batteries**. Ask yourself: What gives me my **strength** and what can I do to feel energetic? What do I need to let go of to make room for growth and new opportunities? It is a time to realign your energy and become aware of what you really want and what is good for you. See this full moon as a **mood booster** that will completely recharge your batteries!

The full moon in Aries is an invitation to focus on the beautiful things in life and on what puts you in a good mood. **Let the warmth and sun´s rays of Aries motivate you!**

AFFIRMATION
FULL MOON IN ARIES

"I IGNITE MY POWER AND TRUST IN MY COURAGE
AND STRENGTH."

FULL MOON
IN ARIES

STRENGTH

COURAGE

SELF-CONFIDENCE

Gemstone:
Red Jasper – Promotes self-confidence and determination

Scents:
Cinnamon, peppermint – energizing scents that strengthen courage

Element: Fire

ACTIVITIES
FOR THE NEXT 2 WEEKS

- Catch some sunlight!
- Get physically active and work up a sweat!
- Try "Somatic Dance"!
- Scream as loud as you can! Maybe into your pillow or go into the forest.

FUN FACT

The October full moon is also known as the **Hunter's Moon**. It represents a time of transition and preparation. During this phase, when nature is slowly preparing for winter, the Hunter's Moon invites us to pause and reflect on what resources we have gathered and what steps to take next. It is a time to gain clarity and prepare for the months ahead. Use its energy to let go of what no longer serves you and gather your strength for the future.

JOURNALLING
FOR THE FULL MOON

REFLECTION QUESTIONS:

- Where have I taken initiative recently?
- What successes have I achieved through my courage?
- What do I need to continue to act confidently?
- When am I impulsive and fiery?
- What gives me strength and energy?

JOURNAL QUESTIONS:

- Am I more resentful or more careless?
- How can I strengthen my initiative in everyday life?
- What does courage mean to me?
- How do I deal with intense feelings and how do I act in extreme moments?

SPACE FOR YOUR ANSWERS:

RITUALS
FULL MOON IN ARIES

Release ritual: Write down the fears that prevent you from being brave. Burn the paper to let go of these fears.

Gratitude ritual: Write down what you are grateful for in your life, especially in terms of courage and initiative.

Mood changer list: Make a list of things that give you energy! Write down everything from listening to music, to catching some sunshine or going for a walk - everything that puts you in a good mood and increases your frequency. Work through this list when you feel powerless and down. It's your personal mood booster!

Contrast showers: Start with warm water and then switch to cold. Start at your feet and slowly work your way up to your legs and arms. Cold water should be used for about 15-30 seconds. Switch to warm water again for 1-2 minutes and finish the cycle with a final cold shower. You can also rinse your face and neck with cold water to increase the invigorating effect. The changes in temperature increases your circulation, strengthens your heart and improves your thermoregulation.

Solar-Plexus-Meditation: Visualise a bright yellow light in your solar plexus giving you energy and courage.

SPACE FOR RITUALS, THOUGHTS, AND NOTES:

21.10.2025
LIBRA
NEW MOON

NEW MOON
IN LIBRA

A gentle breeze of **tranquillity** blows – New Moon in Libra!
This new moon ushers in a time of **balance** and **harmony** that should inspire you to find common ground in your life and **relationships**. Libra, the sign of **partnership** and **alignment**, asks you to find balance between your emotions, between your needs and those of others, and **between giving and taking**. Imagine feeling **calm**, at peace with yourself and centered - that is the feeling we manifest this new moon.

What does this new moon bring?
The new moon in Libra offers you a relaxed new start that floods you with neither too much nor too little energy. It offers you the opportunity to attract and strengthen balance in your professional career, in your relationships - both romantic and platonic- and in your emotional world. Have you perhaps felt tension in your relationships recently or had the feeling that something is out of balance? This new moon gives you the chance to heal these dynamics and find new ways to manifest harmony. At the same time, it is also about balance within yourself - how can you cultivate inner peace and take care of your own well-being? This new moon reminds us not to see everything in black and white!

Focus:
The Libra New Moon asks you to **improve the connections** around you. How do you want to interact with family, friends and strangers? Find your personal balance. How much of the speaking do I do? What is the ratio of give and take? Focus on **fairness** and **equality**. Where in my life do I want more harmony? How can I strengthen my bond with other people while taking good care of myself? This New Moon gives you the opportunity to manifest new partnerships or deepen existing ones. It is also the ideal time to resolve conflicts and create peace, both in your relationships and within yourself.

This new moon invites you to **open your heart to balance and harmony**. It is a wonderful opportunity to find inner peace and foster positive, supportive connections with those around you. Use the powerful energy to manifest ease- within yourself and in your environment.

AFFIRMATION
NEW MOON IN LIBRA

"I MANIFEST HARMONY AND BALANCE IN ALL MY
RELATIONSHIPS AND IN MY LIFE."

NEW MOON
IN LIBRA

RELATIONSHIPS

HARMONY

BALANCE

Gemstone:
Rose Quartz –
Promotes love,
compassion and
harmony

Scents:
Geranium, sandalwood
– calming scents that
support balance and
harmony

Element: Air

DO'S AND DON'TS

✔ Pay attention. Listen sincerely and give your loved ones little joys.

✗ Argumentativeness and conflict. Put yourself in the other person's shoes.

✗ Indecision and hesitation!

ACTIVITIES FOR THE NEXT 4 WEEKS:

- Take a handstand workshop.
- Go rollerblading, ice skating or skateboarding - do something that improves your balance.
- Structure your week so that you have enough time for hobbies, family, friends, your job and yourself.
- Apologise to someone who is long overdue for an apology.

JOURNALLING
TO THE NEW MOON

REFLECTION QUESTIONS:

- What do I need for inner balance?
- Are my relationships and connections balanced or rather one-sided?
- What do I need to be happy to give more than I receive?
- What is easy for me to give and what is difficult for me to give?
- Which relationships are harmonious and balanced, and why?
- What have I learned about balance in my life?

JOURNAL QUESTIONS:

- How can I bring more harmony into my relationships?
- Which aspects of my life need more balance?
- How can I show more compassion and understanding?
- How do I make decisions?
- When do I find it easy and when do I find it difficult to make a decision?

SPACE FOR YOUR ANSWERS:

RITUALS
NEW MOON IN LIBRA

Gratitude ritual: Write down what you are grateful for in your relationships, for example the support of friends or the love of a partner.

Manifestation ritual: Write down what harmony in your relationships should look like and what balance feels like to you in your life. Visualise peaceful, loving interactions with others and a feeling of balance within yourself.

Manifestation task: Create a gift list in your phone notes. Make a note of every time one of your loved ones expresses a wish. Fulfill one of them every now and then!

Heart-Chakra-Meditation: Visualise a bright green light in your heart chakra to help you radiate unconditional love and harmony. Imagine this light filling all your relationships with compassion and understanding.

SPACE FOR RITUALS, THOUGHTS, AND NOTES:

_____
_____
_____
_____
_____
_____
_____
_____
_____
_____
_____
_____
_____
_____
_____
_____
_____
_____
_____
_____
_____
_____
_____

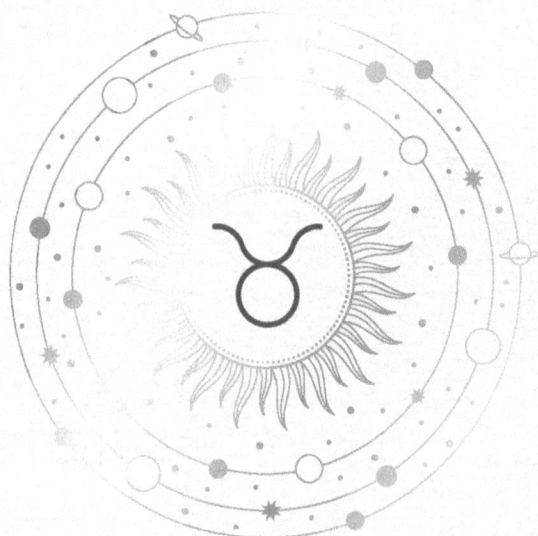

05.11.2025
TAURUS
FULL MOON

FULL MOON
IN TAURUS

The full moon in Taurus brings a strong connection to the themes of **stability** and **sensuality**. It is a time to become aware of the **abundance** around you and to allow yourself to enjoy the **good things** in life.

Taurus is **down-to-earth** and **grounded** and asks you to be the same. Connect with Mother Earth and keep your feet on the ground. However, this does not mean that you cannot still be proud of the path you have taken so far! Do not confuse being down-to-earth with self-denial. You do not have to make yourself smaller than you are, instead show off your magnificent horns with your head held high!

This **solid** yet powerful down-to-earth energy helps you to focus on the **practical aspects of life** and to see your life, **values** and needs more clearly!

What does this full moon bring?

The energy of this moon helps you to separate yourself from external influences and not to let them distract you. It allows you to feel **stable** and **secure** and to let go of all confusion and unrest.

The Taurus always takes the **direct route** - sometimes even banging his head against a wall. But you can always rely on his **commitment**.

Feel how the moon and the universe are having your back! Don't take unnecessary detours towards the future and avoid all distractions to the right and left of your path.

Focus:

The Taurus moon reminds us to **enjoy life**! Leave everything behind that is holding you back. What is stopping you from incorporating sensuality into your everyday life? What stresses you and what gives you peace of mind? Taurus, as an earth sign, calls us to immerse ourselves in our bodies and the world around us. It is a time to connect with the earth, to live life to the fullest and to become aware of what is really important to us. The full moon in Taurus invites us to **appreciate our resources**, enjoy the fruits of our labours and at the same time open ourselves to what is yet to come.

Enjoy the grounded calm of the moon! Enjoy everything, however small or big in your life and listen to your gut feeling!

AFFIRMATION
FULL MOON IN TAURUS

"I GIVE MYSELF SECURITY, TRUST IN MY INNER STRENGTH AND AM PROUD OF MY SUCCESSES SO FAR."

FULL MOON
IN TAURUS

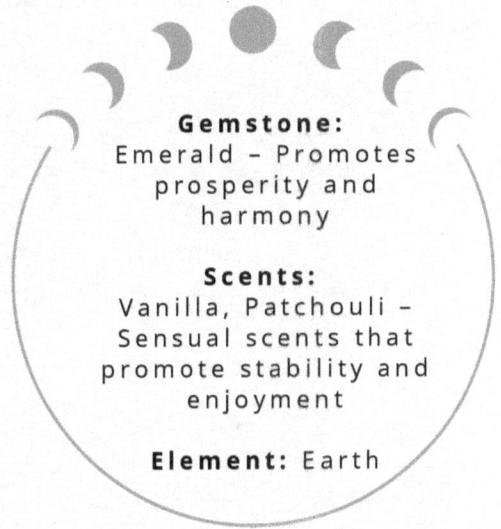

STABILITY

ENJOYMENT

ABUNDANCE

Gemstone:
Emerald – Promotes prosperity and harmony

Scents:
Vanilla, Patchouli – Sensual scents that promote stability and enjoyment

Element: Earth

ACTIVITIES
FOR THE NEXT 2 WEEKS

- Take time for self-care and enjoyment.
- Reflect on your financial and material goals.
- Avoid hectic activities and enjoy the peace and quiet.
- Social media detox: Give yourself a break from social media!
- Go to a fancy gourmet restaurant.

FUN FACT

The full moon in November is also called the **Misty Moon** by Native Americans. The Misty Moon brings a mystical atmosphere as a veil falls over meadows and forests. This gives the landscape a mysterious, almost magical aura. It reminds us that change and growth happen even in times of uncertainty. It is a time to pause, reflect on our own path and have faith in what awaits us in the shadows.

JOURNALLING
FOR THE FULL MOON

REFLECTION QUESTIONS:

- In which areas of life do I feel safe?
- Do I decide and live according to my own values?
- Where have I allowed myself to be influenced by others recently?
- What have I really enjoyed in the last few weeks and what has done me good?
- When was the last time I was in nature?
- Have I spoken kindly to myself lately?

JOURNAL QUESTIONS:

- What does stability and security mean to me?
- How can I strengthen my resilience to feel safe even in the unknown?
- How can I bring more enjoyment into my life?
- What does abundance mean to me?
- What would help me to enjoy my life and find it really great?

SPACE FOR YOUR ANSWERS:

Release ritual: Write down all the fears about the future, the feeling of imperfection and everything that prevents you from feeling fulfilled. Burn the paper to let everything go.

Gratitude ritual: Write down what you are grateful for in your life, especially in terms of possessions, abundance and well-being.

List of achievements: Make a list of your achievements! Write down all of your personal successes, no matter how big or small they are - from calling for a dentist appointment to graduating from college. This list helps you remember everything you have already achieved in difficult moments and builds self-confidence. It is a valuable reminder of how much you have already mastered and motivates you to keep going, even when things get challenging.

Walk a barefoot path and forest bathe: Barefoot paths are made of different materials that provide natural stimulation to the foot reflex zones. Forest bathing is the conscious immersion in the peace and scent of the forest with all of the senses - hearing, seeing, smelling and feeling. Both strengthen the immune system, promote well-being, reduce stress and deepen the connection to nature.

Root-Chakra-Meditation: Visualise a warm, red light in your root chakra. Imagine how this light gives you security, stability and trust. It strengthens your sense of belonging and gives you the strength to stand firm in your life. Let this energy flow through your body and feel how centered and connected to the earth you are.

SPACE FOR RITUALS, THOUGHTS, AND NOTES:

20.11.2025

SCORPIO

NEW MOON

NEW MOON
IN SCORPIO

The New Moon in Scorpio brings a profound, **mystical** and **magical** energy that immerses us in the **transformative power** of this sign. Scorpio calls us to explore our **inner world** and **secrets**, identify hidden **emotions** and **unconscious patterns**, and manifest profound changes. The Scorpio Moon represents **transformation** and gives us the opportunity to **reinvent our inner planet of emotions**. Scorpio, known for its ability to **metamorphose** and **regenerate**, encourages us to connect with our **emotional depth** and discover the hidden parts of our soul.

What does this new moon bring?
This new moon gives us **meaningful access to ourselves** and our subconscious. Use this time to cultivate **emotional intimacy** with yourself. The power of this moon gives us the opportunity to capture and manifest our deepest desires and intentions. It invites us to **embrace the darkness** and explore the hidden aspects of our souls. Use this new moon to find out what you really want. It is the moment to recognise your **deepest mysteries** and admit to yourself what you may not have believed you could do or what you have not allowed yourself to do. What has prevented you from accessing your secret desires so far? And what is mentally holding you back from fulfilling them? **Accept the dark sides of yourself, accept old wounds and use the abundance of your feelings to make your wishes come true.**

Focus:
Awaken your inner alchemist! Now is the time to use your subconscious to your advantage, reprogram it and open yourself to the magic of transformation. Use rituals or meditations to set your intentions and celebrate your emotional shift. Let the power of the new moon in Scorpio inspire you to **integrate your shadows** and **fully accept yourself**. Invite even more **spirituality**, **witchcraft** and the **magic of the universe** into your everyday life. Unite your inner witch and your inner goddess and realise that you have always been one. Become aware of your magic and your infinite potential! Prepare yourself for a deep **emotional realignment** and open yourself to the possibility of living your true self.

Feel the tingling in your fingertips because miracles are waiting for you. Be ready because the universe can't wait for you to live and celebrate your essence! Now is the time to enter this **revolutionary phase** with intention and trust - your new chapter is waiting for you. **Let your shadow dance with your light and you will be unstoppable!**

AFFIRMATION
NEW MOON IN SCORPIO

"I MANIFEST DEEP EMOTIONAL HEALING AND
ALLOW MYSELF TO EXPERIENCE TRUE INTIMACY."

♏

NEW MOON
IN SCORPIO

◇ SECRETS

TRANSFORMATION

INTIMACY

Gemstone:
Obsidian – Supports
inner healing and
protection

Scents:
Patchouli, Myrrh –
Earthy, profound
scents that promote
transformation and
letting go.

Element: Water

DOS AND DONTS

✓ Open up! Share a secret with someone you care about. It will definitely feel easier afterwards.

✗ Pay attention to your vibrations: Don't be jealous, resentful or too critical.

✗ Everyone makes mistakes. Own up to them and don't be stubborn!

ACTIVITIES FOR THE NEXT 4 WEEKS:

- Spend time in deep self-reflection and meditation.
- Work on building deep, honest connections with others.
- Smudge yourself and your home!
- Take care of your vitamin and hormone levels. Get informed and possibly buy supplements, teas or oils.
- Go to a thermal bath, a spa or go swimming.

JOURNALLING
FOR THE NEW MOON

REFLECTION QUESTIONS:

- What transformations have I experienced in the last few weeks?
- Was I able to share my inner, deepest truth with those around me?
- How have my relationships changed in terms of intimacy?
- What have I learned about emotional healing and letting go?
- When did I feel most connected to myself?

JOURNAL QUESTIONS:

- Which emotional patterns do I want to let go of and transform?
- How can I build deeper connections with others and with myself?
- What does true intimacy mean to me?
- Where do I need more intimacy and emotional healing?
- How does my spiritual journey feel to me?

SPACE FOR YOUR ANSWERS:

RITUALS
NEW MOON IN SCORPIO

Gratitude Ritual: Write down what you are grateful for in your emotional life, especially in relation to healing and transformation that you have already experienced.

Manifestation Ritual: Write down what emotional transformations you want to manifest in your life. Visualise yourself healing old wounds and developing deeper intimacy with yourself and others.

Manifestation task: Manifest small, everyday events every day - like finding a feather, a penny or a parking space right in front of your workplace. Mini-manifestations are a powerful way to experience the principle of manifestation in everyday life. The approach is the same as always: you imagine what you want, visualise the desired result and experience the feeling you would have if it were already true - this feeling can also simply be a joyfully surprising one. Then you let it go. It is therefore best to write down your mini-manifestations in the evening before going to bed: what do you want to manifest, the feeling and the date of fulfilment. They show you that you have the power to shape your reality and at the same time reveal where you may be making mistakes - for example, if you cannot let go or are too attached to a certain result. Practice makes perfect!

Sacral-Chakra-Meditation: Visualise a bright orange light in your sacral chakra to help you experience emotional depth and intimacy. Imagine this light giving you emotional security and showing you that you are whole and held.

SPACE FOR RITUALS, THOUGHTS, AND NOTES:

05.12.2025
GEMINI
FULL MOON

FULL MOON
IN GEMINI

The **last full moon** of 2025 shines in the sign of Gemini and brings just the right energy for the **sociable** and **family-oriented** festive season.

The sign's **sociability** and **adaptability** help us to be **flexible** and **open** in our dealings with others. This moon reminds us that each of us has good and bad traits and asks us to view the behaviour of others more casually and with more ease. **Seek open and loving conversations!** Every conversation teaches us something valuable and leaves us with insights to carry forward.

What does this full moon bring?

The full moon in Gemini brings a refreshing energy of **communication** and **exchange**. This moon invites you to **deepen conversations**, **discover new perspectives** and **strengthen connections**. It is the perfect moment to clear up misunderstandings and create **lightheartedness** in your relationships. The Gemini energy offers you the opportunity to overcome communication difficulties with the people you love. Things that have remained unsaid can now be resolved. Let go of old problems that have stood between you and use the power of this moon to be honest and understanding. The Gemini full moon not only promotes the ease of exchange, but also the desire to improve and strengthen relationships.

Focus:

This full moon is about appreciating the **diversity** of this year! Life is worth living, thanks to all its different facets. **Be grateful** for your experiences, your adaptability and the changes you have lived through. This full moon wants you to become aware of everything you have learned this year and challenges you to broaden your knowledge even further. **Celebrate variety, diversity and complexity!**

The Gemini full moon encourages us to let go of everything that keeps us from having an **effortless and uncomplicated festive season**. It reminds us that not every day has to be the same and to celebrate diversity!

AFFIRMATION
FULL MOON GEMINI

"I OPEN MY MIND TO NEW KNOWLEDGE AND SHARE
MY THOUGHTS WITH EASE."

♊

FULL MOON
IN GEMINI

Gemstone:
Fluorite – Promotes mental clarity and strengthens the ability to process information quickly

Scents:
Lemon, mint – invigorating scents that refresh the mind

Element: Air

COMMUNICATION

VERSATILITY

LEARNING

ACTIVITIES
FOR THE NEXT 2 WEEKS

- Find a hobby that complements your other interests. For example, if you're already active in sports, try something creative - or vice versa.
- Write a blog or share your thoughts.
- Be curious and try to learn something from every conversation!
- Join a family member's hobby to strengthen a bond and broaden your horizons.
- Go to markets with your loved ones!

FUN FACT

The **Winter Moon**, also called the **Cold Moon**, is the last full moon of the year. It symbolises the time of retreat and reflection as nature goes into hibernation. Even though the days are short, this moon encourages us to celebrate our successes and moments of light from the past year. It reminds us that after every dark period, the sun comes again. Use the energy of this full moon for introspection and to rest. The name "Cold Moon" was given by Native American tribes, who used this term because of the harsh, cold winter conditions during this time.

JOURNALLING
FOR THE FULL MOON

REFLECTION QUESTIONS:

- What have I learned about myself or others?
- Where do I have gaps in my knowledge that I would like to fill in?
- What topics do I find challenging to approach with understanding, openness, and flexibility, and why?
- What were my "firsts" for this year?
- Have I had loving, clear and open communication recently?
- Where have I felt heavy lately and how can I bring more ease into these aspects?

JOURNAL QUESTIONS:

- What topics interest me?
- How can I bring more diversity into my life?
- What does "successful conversation" mean to me?
- What does connection mean to me and how can I strengthen it?
- What stops me from being curious?
- What does lightheartedness mean to me? How can I bring ease into my life?

SPACE FOR YOUR ANSWERS:

RITUALS
FULL MOON IN GEMINI

Release ritual: Write down which old ways of thinking or communication patterns you want to let go of. Burn the paper safely.

Gratitude ritual: Write down the learning achievements, skills, conversations and communication skills you are grateful for.

Set a goal : Set yourself a new learning goal or challenge that inspires you. Acquire a new skill or complete exciting courses that expand your knowledge.

Create a book list: A book list is an overview of books you have read or still want to read. It helps you organise your reading progress, record important content and ensure that you don't forget any inspiring books that you really wanted to read. Write down 1. the start date, 2. the date you finished reading a book, 3. the title and 4. the most important findings. You can enter books that you still want to read directly into the title list and add to them later. This way you can keep track of your reading habits and goals.

Throat-Chakra-Meditation: Visualise a clear, sky blue light in your throat chakra. This light opens your channel for honest communication and strengthens your ability to express your truth.

SPACE FOR RITUALS, THOUGHTS, AND NOTES:

20.12.2025

SAGITTARIUS
NEW MOON

NEW MOON
IN SAGITTARIUS

How time flies - It is the **last new moon** of 2025: The Sagittarius new moon arrives with a burst of **excitement** and boundless **joy**!

Sagittarius stands for **freedom**, **curiosity** and **expansion** – perfect for starting the new year with **fire** and **motivation**!

During the homely Christmas days, the new moon offers us the opportunity to celebrate the last days of the year with our loved ones and to philosophise about visions of the future. It asks us to think about future adventures, **wishes** and **experiences**. Sagittarius seems to take life lightly. They are not afraid of any new start, **change** or challenge and even enjoy being outside of their comfort zone. With this **fearless** energy, the transformation between the years is particularly easy!

What does this new moon bring?

The new moon in Sagittarius brings a good dose of **fearlessness**, **fun** and a thirst for **adventure**. The fiery energy turns Christmas into a party and then truly kicks off on New Year's Eve. **Be impulsive, loud and bursting with happiness!** Sagittarius can do anything except be boring. So let your childlike side come out and enjoy the time with those closest to you! Be open to ideas, flashes of inspiration and sudden insights. This new moon is not afraid of anything, so take this breeze of **carefreeness**, **heroism** and **zest for life** with you and plant your first visions for 2026 without wavering!

Focus:

The new moon in Sagittarius gives you the tools to lay the foundation for the next year. It invites you to **think outside the box** and find ways to start your expedition of **personal growth**. Perhaps you have long wanted to **travel**, get to know new cultures or learn new skills - now is the moment to plan the first steps, perhaps with a little recklessness! Let your **passion** for the unknown and your longing for freedom flow into your life. The new moon in Sagittarius opens the doors to **new opportunities** and **adventures** that are just waiting to be discovered by you!

End the year 2025 with fun and childlike anticipation of the future. **Dance, laugh** and start the year 2026 with a **good mood** and **high frequency**! Get ready to be the best version of yourself! But for now, enjoy the here and now. You deserve it!

The universe wishes you happy holidays and a happy new year!

AFFIRMATION
NEW MOON IN SAGITTARIUS

"I MANIFEST FREEDOM AND JOY IN ALL AREAS OF MY LIFE."

NEW MOON
IN SAGITTARIUS

FREEDOM

EXPANSION

JOY OF LIFE

Gemstone:
Lapis Lazuli – Promotes wisdom and spiritual expansion

Scents:
Cedar, Pine – Refreshing scents that support clarity and a sense of adventure

Element: Fire

DOS AND DONTS

✓ Say yes! Don't be afraid to try things you haven't yet. You are allowed to be crazy sometimes.

✗ Don't let fear hold you back! Fear is the best advisor to show you the end of your comfort zone - and then leave it anyway!

ACTIVITIES FOR THE NEXT 4 WEEKS:

- Celebrate the year 2025! Find or throw a gigantic New Year's Eve party.
- Give the gift of experiences, adventures, or travel plans this Christmas. Time spent together is the most precious gift you can offer!
- Dance with your loved ones under the Christmas tree, play games and have fun!
- Buy tickets for a festival or a concert.
- Avoid excessive demands, restlessness and tactlessness. Family members can be triggers - make sure you are not one of them!

JOURNALLING
FOR THE NEW MOON

REFLECTION QUESTIONS:

- What goals did I achieve in the past year?
- Which adventures and experiences were particularly exciting?
- What title would I give to the year 2025?
- What support do I have?
- Where have I particularly developed myself this year?
- Where have I recently experienced a sense of freedom and expansion?

JOURNAL QUESTIONS:

- What childlike aspects do I see in myself, that I like or dislike?
- Which places in this world do I still want to see?
- What's on my bucket list?
- What moments are outside my comfort zone, and how can I change that?
- How do I want to develop myself next year?
- What are my 3 biggest goals for 2026?
- What challenges do I want to face?

SPACE FOR YOUR ANSWERS:

_____

_____

_____

_____

_____

_____

_____

_____

_____

_____

_____

_____

_____

_____

_____

_____

_____

_____

RITUALS
NEW MOON IN SAGITTARIUS

Gratitude Ritual: Write down what you are grateful for in relation to freedom, past travels and adventures, and personal growth.

Manifestation Ritual: Write down your professional and personal goals, desired adventures, and experiences. Distinguish between short-term goals for the next 4 weeks and long-term goals for the upcoming year 2026. Visualise how you achieve these goals with enthusiasm and courage, exploring new horizons along the way.

Manifestation Task: Create a vision board for the year 2026 that ignites your fire and motivation every time you look at it. It doesn't have to be perfect or complete. You can add to it and modify it at any time.

Crown-Chakra-Meditation: Visualise a glowing, violet light shining at your crown chakra at the top of your head. This light connects you with universal wisdom and your higher self. Feel yourself opening up to divine inspiration and deep trust in the flow of life. Imagine this light bringing you joy, a sense of adventure, and a broad perspective on all the possibilities ahead of you.

SPACE FOR RITUALS, THOUGHTS AND NOTES:

More space for ideas, letters, compliments, successes, dreams or plans:

MY MINI MANIFESTATIONS

WHAT?	FEELING:	DATE

MY BOOK-LIST

TITLE	CONTENT	READ FROM TO

MY LIST OF
MOOD CHANGER

1.

2.

3.

4.

5.

6.

7.

8.

9.

10.

This Moon Calendar 2025 is dedicated to the themes of spirituality, moon rituals, and astrology from the personal perspective of the author. It aims to inspire the reader towards self-reflection and individual growth. The content is designed to offer insights and create space for personal rituals and inner contemplation.

THANK YOU!

From the bottom of my heart, I thank you for holding my Moon Calendar 2025 in your hands and supporting my first book and passion project. It means the world to me that I've had the privilege of accompanying you a little on your journey.

I hope that my soul has touched yours, and that the pages of this book have offered you inspiration, joy, and perhaps a little bit of magic. If we all invite just a bit more magic into this world, may it become even more colourful, peaceful, mindful, and loving—a place where we can each arrive more fully within ourselves.

It would bring me so much joy if you could share your experience with this book in an online review or recommend it to others to inspire them to connect with the beautiful energy of the moon.

Thank you for being a part of this journey.

With love and a pinch of magic,

NADINE

Imprint

Nadine Fuhr © Copyright - All rights reserved
Auf dem Lehnacker 13a, 56132 Frücht
fuhrnadine@web.de
ISBN: 9798301515347
1st Edition 2024
Printed by Amazon Germany or partner

Made in United States
Troutdale, OR
02/06/2025

28712503R00146